1981

THE UNITY OF
THE FAERIE QUEENE

SOUTH ATLANTIC
MODERN LANGUAGE ASSOCIATION
AWARD STUDY

THE UNITY OF

The Faerie Queene

RONALD ARTHUR HORTON

THE UNIVERSITY OF GEORGIA PRESS

ATHENS

Copyright © 1978 by the University of Georgia Press
Athens 30602

All rights reserved

Set in 12 on 12½ point Mergenthaler Garamond type
Printed in the United States of America

Library of Congress Cataloging in Publication Data

Horton, Ronald Arthur, 1936–
    The unity of The faerie queene.
    (South Atlantic Modern Language Association award
study)
    Includes bibliographical references and index.
    1. Spenser, Edmund, 1552?–1599. Faerie queene.   I.
Title.   II. Series: South Atlantic Modern Language Association. Award study.
PR2358.H58   821'.3   77–15793
        ISBN 0–8203–0440–9

Nor is a very large animal beautiful (for then one's view does not occur all at once, but, rather, the unity and wholeness of the animal are lost to the viewer's sight as would happen, for example, if we should come across an animal a thousand miles in length).

Aristotle, *The Poetics,* vii

Contents

Preface

The following study makes a case for the unity of *The Faerie Queene* in terms of general structures indicated in Spenser's prefatory Letter to Sir Walter Raleigh. Its divisions are intended as phases of an argument rather than as exegeses of particular segments or aspects of the poem. *Faerie Queene* criticism now abounds with close readings of particular incidents but has been slow to show their articulation in the general scheme. Insofar as the scheme is already recognized, this argument will traverse what for the informed Spenserian is familiar territory. Traversing this territory is necessary, however, if the study is to have value for the uninitiated. It is also necessary for the integrity of the argument, for undocumented critical and historical commonplaces are vulnerable in an era of revisionism in Spenser studies. An argument that consists, in part, of extending the implications of the known must not only restate the known for the uninitiated but also certify it for the well-informed when it supports a superstructure of interpretation.

It is a pleasure to acknowledge the persons and institutions that have assisted this work. A Folger Shakespeare Library summer fellowship facilitated the research, and the continuing generosity of Bob Jones University enabled the writing to proceed in the midst of professional responsibilities. The book has benefited by the close attention of Jerry Leath Mills of the University of North Carolina and the advice of my colleagues Stewart Custer and Guenter Salter. A special debt is due to O. B. Hardison, Jr., Director of the Folger Shakespeare Library, who originally suggested to me the importance of the larger structures of *The Faerie*

Queene and encouraged me to look for clues to its unifying principles in the Letter to Raleigh, at a time in my professional growth when it seemed safer to assume the value of the subtle than of the obvious and of the unconscious than of the stated intention. The ability to discuss without embarrassment ideal virtue I owe to my parents, who taught by their example the possibility of the ideal and by precept the necessity to "add to your faith virtue" (2 Pet. 1:5). Of fortitude the supreme exemplar is my wife, Martha Dillard Horton, to whom this book is gratefully dedicated.

THE UNITY OF
THE FAERIE QUEENE

INTRODUCTION

The Letter and the Poem

The question of unity has been more central in the criticism of *The Faerie Queene* than in the critical histories of most works of literature. The problem of unity entailed by its fragmentary form is aggravated by three circumstances: (1) the length of the part that does exist, (2) the requirement of the plan according to which it remained for the last book to present the occasion of the twelve quests and to coordinate their relations, and (3) some discrepancies between the plan announced in Spenser's Letter to Sir Walter Raleigh and followed generally, and certain details of the poem. These difficulties have caused critics since the seventeenth century to question the structural integrity of the poem, and though recent defenses of the poem's unity are not lacking, most do not argue for the design explained in the Letter.

Critical dissatisfaction with this design has been of three kinds: disintegrationist, organicist, and mimeticist. The disintegrationist view finds fault with the coherence of the plan or with the consistency with which it was carried out or with both. Neoclassical critics debated whether the Arthur story is prominent enough to impart the required unity of action, and the consensus up to the present has been that Arthur's quest is neither sufficiently dominant nor sufficiently well integrated with the other adventures to provide effective unity. After Thomas Rymer, the formlessness (by classical standards) of the plot was commonly attributed to the influence of Ariosto, and the Ariostan model was polarized with the Aristotelian dicta as the opposing influences responsible for the disunity of the poem. In 1762 Bishop Hurd's defense of *The Faerie Queene* on principles of "gothic" unity prepared the way for a view of the poem as unsuccessfully combining two conflicting types of structure. Hurd, having stressed the need for judging the unity of *The Faerie Queene* according to nonclassical criteria, conceded that the quest of Arthur for Gloriana was a classical expedient foisted upon the essentially "gothic" design of the poem. The theory of the two structures was not carried forward until early in this century, when W. L. Renwick observed that Spenser's intention to "overgo" Ariosto consisted in his plan to compensate for the amorphousness of the romance by adding the structural firmness of the epic and that the origin of Spenser's notion was his reading in the Italian critics of his time, who had argued the practicability of such a synthesis.[1] Most recently, W.J.B. Owen, in a detailed analysis of the form of *The Faerie Queene,* has distinguished two conflicting structures: the epic (the story of Arthur) and the repetitive (the quests of the knights). In addition, Josephine Waters Bennett, to whom Owen is indebted, has called attention to two "rival focis of narrative"—Arthur's quest and Cleopolis—producing the incongruity of opposing currents of narrative movement, toward and away from Gloriana's court and yet somehow fusing as Arthur joins the other knights in their adventures.[2] Thus there appears not only an opposition of Ariostan and Aristotelian influences, but even within the explicit, deliberately executed design, a conflict between the encompassing quest of Arthur and the serial quests of the titular knights.

In the late nineteenth century, with R. W. Church, the idea emerged that the conflicting structures, and especially the discrepancies between the Letter to Raleigh and the poem, are evidence of a change in plan. The Letter was assumed to represent the original plan that Spenser abandoned, either from an awareness of its defects or from the influence of Ariosto. R.E.N. Dodge, Ernest de Selincourt, and Herbert Cory in the early twentieth century accepted this view, Cory suggesting that it was the death of Leicester

that scuttled the original plan (*Variorum,* 1:343–44). Janet
Spens saw in the discrepancies evidence of revision but
believed that the Letter represents the later plan. J. H.
Walter and Josephine Bennett agreed, and Bennett offered
detailed support to the revision theory in her influential
study *The Evolution of "The Faerie Queene."*[3] The most recent
attempt to chart the growth of *The Faerie Queene* from the
discrepancies noticed by Bennett and others is that of
W.J.B. Owen, who regards the Letter as a statement of
Spenser's intention to revise the scheme of the poem shortly
before the publication of the first installment in 1590.
Because of the exigencies of publication, this revision,
Owen suggests, was never fully carried out; consequently
the earlier Ariostan manner remains in Book III. In writing
the next installment, Spenser, realizing the impracticability
of the plan stated in the Letter, drew again upon the
Arisostan material for Book IV to finish what he had begun
in Book III. It is easy to understand why the main current of
Faerie Queene criticism—the disintegrationist—has been
disheartening to many readers. The poem has been generally regarded as lacking a clear central idea or narrative
thrust, combining unsuccessfully two or more conflicting
structures, and remaining an awkward composite of at least
two distinct stages of revision. Spenser's art, remarks Bennett, is like that of the medieval stained glass window:
"Spenser created lovely bits and fitted them together with
great skill, but the general structure, the connecting frame
of lead and iron, is hardly strong enough to support the
weight of colored glass" (pp. 106–7).

In the organicist view of the poem, the discreteness of the
parts is nothing to be regretted. Since Thomas Warton's
Observations on the Fairy Queen of Spenser (1752), romantic
critics have found *The Faerie Queene* quite to their liking for
the very reasons that other critics have been ill at ease with
it. Warton explained, with evident satisfaction, that "Spenser . . . did not live in an age of planning" and that his

poetry must be appreciated as "the careless exuberance of a warm imagination and a strong sensibility" (*Variorum,* 1:320). Succeeding generations of romantic readers including William Hazlitt, James Russell Lowell, and William Butler Yeats have welcomed the results of disintegrationist analysis and dispensed with the whole issue of schematic unity in savoring the sensuousness and pageantry of particular scenes. According to Ernest de Selincourt, echoing Coleridge, we are compensated for the lack of a clear direction and certain destination by the pleasures of the journey.[4] Other analogies have been pressed into service to veil the apparent structural inadequacy of the poem while conveying an impression of continuity. Lowell's analogy of the splendid gallery of pictures has proved durable, but more often we are invited to consider the poem's coherence as that of a tapestry or of a dream.[5] Recent formalist criticism tends to focus on the fictional, mythic, or iconic vehicle rather than on theme and argues for less obtrusive fictional or symbolic coherence. It characteristically regards the poem as complete in its present state or as "theoretically endless" and as having assumed its shape under the governance of what E.M.W. Tillyard has called an "unconscious structural tact."[6]

In recent organicist criticism, the bias against schematic unity and traditional didacticism is given a mimetic rationale. Its minimizing the importance of the scheme of the virtues is a consequence not only of romantic antirationalism and aestheticism but also of the association of artistic integrity with an honest imitation of life and an honest imitation of life with an existential cosmos. Modern mimeticist criticism finds implicit structure more congenial to the reflection of the amorphousness of human experience and a nonjudgmental stance more in keeping with ethical relativity. Thus critics as diverse in their approaches and assumptions as Harry Berger, Jr., and Paul Alpers find the unity of the poem not in the scheme of the virtues but in the psychological drama of a maturing consciousness, with crude simplistic concepts gradually giving way to a proper appreciation of the complexity of life and a willingness to settle for partial solutions to human problems. For these and other critics, the lengthening shadows of disillusionment provide a satisfying sense of completion as the moral awareness of the poet or of the reader or of the fictional consciousness immanent in the poem aligns with the impressions of the modern mind. A poem ostensibly concerned with the moral education of an Elizabethan gentleman in the traditional Christian and humanistic virtues turns out to be, in effect, a proleptic allegorical *bildungsroman*. Its coherence, like that of the world of modern scientism, is one of process rather than that of a closed system. This view of the unity of *The Faerie Queene* is determined partially, it is fair to say, by the accumulated weight of argument by generations of disintegrationist critics but also by extrinsic factors: the preference of organic to mechanic form and the extrapolation of modern pessimism into the past.

The critical approach that has produced the most startling results of all recent discussions of the poem's unity is numerological analysis. Though sometimes unconvincing, Alastair Fowler has produced impressive support for the preexistence of a precisely articulating scheme that Spenser was gradually filling in. The discovery of an intricate pattern of number symbolism controlling the content of books, cantos, and sometimes even stanzas militates strongly against the usual view of *The Faerie Queene* as having evolved somewhat haphazardly and, in essential respects, unconsciously into its present form. Architectonic unity appears to be a feature of the poem that Spenser took very seriously and upon which he exercised a great deal of care.[7]

If *The Faerie Queene* shows evidence of having been formed according to a preconceived plan, the obvious place to look for such a plan is the controversial "Letter of the Authors expounding his whole intention in the course of this worke." The content of the Letter to Raleigh has been variously regarded as a valid, accurate statement of the plan being followed in the poem; an original but abandoned plan; a partially executed plan of revision; a reader's guide to the first installment of a poem begun in medias res; a preliminary archetype after which Spenser was more or less faithfully modeling his poem; a historiographer's, as distinct from a poet's, account; and an unaccountable untruth. To many critics it is an obstacle in salvaging the poem for modern sensibility. Combining the fallacies and heresies eschewed by the New Criticism with a simplistic moral classification, it affronts the critical and moral intelligence of today's sophisticated reader. To critics less concerned with reconciling Spenser to modern sensibility and perhaps more readily disposed to allow at least the historical validity of its aesthetic and ethical premises, the Letter to Raleigh offers, despite some difficulties, a useful account of the poem. William Nelson is convinced that Spenser's statements of intention in the Letter, as well as in the poem itself, "are designed to give 'great light to the Reader' rather than to mislead him" and that they deserve, therefore, to be taken on faith rather than summarily rejected. More astringently, Robert Ellrodt observes that "a needless expense of ingenuity would have been spared, had not some critics thought they knew what Spenser meant better than he knew himself. For once, the safest method is to abide by the Letter of the Authors expounding his whole intention in the course of this worke." Alastair Fowler, while arguing for numerological underpinning, sees "no reason to question" the statement in the Letter. In fact, he remarks, the twelve-book scheme was an obvious numerological choice, for epics "imitated the entire zodiac of life." The conclusion of the planetary week with Book VII does not imply the conclusion of the poem; Spenser merely capitalizes on its value as a supplementary structure in the Mutability Cantos.[8] The Letter to Raleigh merits a much closer examination and comparison with the poem than it has generally received, if only because it was, one may presume, an honest attempt by the author to enlighten the reader. Moreover, one need not assume that the author's conscious and unconscious intentions necessarily worked at cross-purposes.

Of the charges against the accuracy of the Letter, the most persistent and serious are three: the limited role of Arthur, the divergence of Books III and IV from the quest pattern, and the contradictory accounts of the origins of Guyon's and Scudamour's quests. The impression that *The Faerie Queene* is not really about Arthur has caused many critics to dispense with the explanation offered in the Letter. Indeed Spenser makes little use of the traditional Arthurian materials; his central figure is Arthur before he became king. Rosamund Tuve has pointed out that the sixteenth-century reader familiar with the Vulgate Cycle of romances or with Malory would not have expected a more prominent fictional role for Arthur. Arthur, though not dominant, was "fundamental" in the adventures of the knights of his court, and his glory and the health of his kingdom were bound up in their successes or failures. Spenser's Arthur, like Malory's, "is more important to structure and design than to the flow of the narrative."[9] This structural importance, as well as the greater fictional prominence of the titular knights, is clearly indicated in the Letter. Therefore whatever contradiction may appear to exist in the conception and execution of Arthur's role is not between the Letter and the poem but within each of them.

The same is true of the contention that Books III and IV do not conform to the quest pattern set forth in the Letter. The Letter makes clear that the patron knight of Chastity is not the knight to whom the quest of Book III was originally assigned. The contradiction is not between the Letter and the poem but is contained within both. Book IV is not treated in the plot outline given in the Letter, but we may presume that if Spenser was not embarrassed by the deviation of Book III from the general scheme, he was not in the case of Book IV.

Of the discrepancies between the plot outline and the poetic narrative that are commonly urged against the accuracy of the Letter, the most formidable and frequently cited is the contradiction in the accounts of the origin of Guyon's quest.[10] Book II, canto i, has Guyon's quest occasioned by the discovery of the dead Mordant, the dying Amavia, and the babe with bloody hands. In the Letter, however, the quest is occasioned by the Palmer's presentation of the babe at Fairy Court. Clearly there is a notable discrepancy. It is significant, however, that reflections of the version in the Letter appear later in Book II, when Guyon recounts first to Britomart (ii.42–44) and then to Arthur the story "Of false *Acrasia,* and her wicked wiles, / Which to auenge, the Palmer him forth drew / From Faery court" (ix.9). Evidently the contradiction exists within the poem rather than simply between the Letter and the poem.

The account of the origin of Scudamour's quest for Amoret as it is given in the Letter has been alleged to conflict with the poetic version of the occasion that appears at the beginning of Book IV. In the Letter, on the third day of Gloriana's feast a groom came to court and complained of Busirane's captivity of Amoret, "Whereupon Sir Scudamour the louer of that Lady presently tooke on him that aduenture." In the opening stanzas of Book IV we are told that Amoret was stolen away on her wedding day during the bridal feast. But since we are not told in the poem when Scudamour took up the quest, the two accounts might conceivably be reconciled.

The unresolvable contradictions exist within the Letter or within the poem or within both, not between the Letter and the poem. Therefore it is not justifiable to discredit the Letter on the basis of its divergence from the poem. Whether the fictional inconsistencies are blemishes on the poem is another argument entirely. One may be persuaded, as Josephine Bennett evidently came to be, that allegorical intention takes precedence over narrative consistency.[11] Perhaps, as William Nelson suggests, Spenser did not really care enough about the loose ends of his narrative to tidy up in his revision (pp. 146–47). Graham Hough in a note on the "First Commentary on *The Faerie Queene*," a privately annotated copy of the first edition, observes that the annotator was very much alive to the moral and historical allegory—identifying Red Cross as both Leicester and Christ—but unresponsive to the narrative as fiction.[12] A later student of Spenser, Thomas Warton, writing when literary taste was beginning to shift, observed it as a flaw "that after one of the twelve knights has atchieved the adventure of his proper book, the poet introduces him, in the next book, acting perhaps in an inferior sphere, and degraded to some less dangerous exploit."[13] Warton's objection does not prove that Spenser was a careless craftsman; it may indicate that Spenser was more concerned with allegorical development than with the fictional unity of his character's careers. Fictional unity and consistency were evidently not the measure by which the sixteenth-century reader judged the coherence of *The Faerie Queene,* and we may presume they are not the criteria by which the author might feel we would do the greatest justice to the unity of his poem. Even were the alleged discrepancies between the Letter to Raleigh and the poem possible to demonstrate, they would still not be sufficient to discredit the Letter for the reader chiefly interested in the allegory. And if there be no actual contradiction, even the modern reader may well take a fresh look at the Letter as a guide to the poem, "which otherwise may happily seeme tedious and confused."

Prompting the present study was the impression that the difficulties of length and incompleteness that made the Letter to Raleigh necessary to the readers of the first installment of 1590 and useful to those of the second installment of 1596 (though it did not in fact appear with this edition) have been compounded by the tendency of recent criticism to focus on particular parts and features of the poem rather than on its general structures. These structures, despite Paul Alpers's assurances, are easily missed by the microscopic view.[14] To approach the vast frame of the poem on New Critical principles is to stand in the shadow of what may seem to modern sensibility not unlike Aristotle's animal a thousand miles long, an animal, moreover, without its hindquarters and with some of its parts rather mutilated by what a noted Renaissance scholar has inadvertently denominated "the whole cannon of Spenser criticism." To perceive its lineaments requires the macroscopic view: the comprehensive scope of the distanced and unaided vision—unaided, that is, except by such clarification as the poet has provided in consideration of the fragmentary state of the poem. To reveal these contours is at once to uphold the sincerity and accuracy of Spenser's statement of intention and, more importantly, to rescue the work on its own terms from the opprobrium of formal confusion.

PART I

THE GROUND PLAN:
A NURSERY OF VIRTUE

Than the childes courage, inflamed by the frequent redynge of noble poetes, dayly more and
more desireth to haue experience in those
thinges, that they write of.

Thomas Elyot, *The Governour,* I.x

I · *The Nurturing of an Exemplar*

The conviction of Renaissance critics and poets like Philip Sidney that poetry is superior to philosophy in moving men to virtue through example is reflected in Spenser's description of Arthur in the Letter to Raleigh: "The generall end therefore of all the booke is to fashion a gentleman or noble person in vertuous and gentle discipline." It is in keeping with Renaissance didacticism to construe "fashion" not only as "represent" or "delineate" in reference to Arthur but also as "educate" or "train" in reference to the reader.[1] The effect of the poet's imagination, says Sidney, "is not wholie imaginatiue, as we are wont to say by them that build Castles in the ayre: but so farre substantially it worketh, not onely to make a *Cyrus,* which had been but a particular excellencie, as Nature might haue done, but to bestow a *Cyrus* vpon the worlde, to make many *Cyrus's,* if they wil learne aright why and how that Maker made him."[2] The special property and true function of poetry is to form in the reader the image of virtue that has been formed by the poet in his fictional example.

The description of Arthur in the Letter, as well as in Book I, canto ix, reinforces his identification with the reader. Spenser, like Xenophon, has portrayed an attainable ideal: Arthur, "whome I conceiue after his long education by Timon, to whom he was by Merlin deliuered to be brought vp, so soone as he was borne of the Lady Igrayne, to haue seene in a dream or vision the Faery Queen, with whose excellent beauty rauished, he awaking resolued to seeke her out, and so being by Merlin armed, and by Timon throughly instructed, he went to seeke her forth in Faerye land." Arthur has had a thorough education in the precepts of moral philosophy from his tutor Timon before his vision of Gloriana arouses in him a compelling desire to seek its fulfillment in Fairyland. The reader, a youth of gentle birth with a long education in precepts, sees in Spenser's heroic image an embodiment of his highest potentialities, and allured by the power of poetry he pursues his vision of moral perfection, through emulation of that example, in Fairyland. Poetry, in the reader's moral education, finishes the work of philosophy.

The designs of poetry upon the reader furnish the design of the poem. These designs are implicit in the virtue Arthur is said by Spenser to represent: "So in the person of Prince Arthure I sette forth magnificence in particular, which vertue for that (according to Aristotle and the rest) it is the perfection of all the rest, and conteineth in it them all, therefore in the whole course I mention the deedes of Arthure applyable to that vertue, which I write of in that booke." Rosamund Tuve has shown that Spenser's magnificence is not Aristotle's, nor is it a mistake for magnanimity; its roots are Ciceronian and Macrobian (pp. 57–60). Cicero makes magnificence a branch of fortitude and defines it as "the contemplation and execution of great and sublime projects with a certain grandeur and magnificence of imagination."[3] In Macrobius's list of virtues associated with fortitude, magnificence is followed by *constantia, tolerantia,* and *firmitas.* In later lists Cicero's *patientia* commonly replaced *tolerantia* as the virtue associated with Christ's willingness to endure persecution and hardship. Alanus's list adds Cicero's *perseverantia* to Macrobius's list. As a consequence of the mutual influence of these branches of the cardinal virtue fortitude and the synthesizing of the lists by later writers, magnificence frequently took on both the meanings of high achievement and endurance to the end. Thus in the *Somme le roi,* as translated in the *Book of Virtues and Vices,* both meanings appear: "Þe sixte degree of douȝtynesse þei clepen magnificence, þat is grete hiȝenesse.

Þis vertue þei deuisen on þis wise: magnificence, þei seien, is of hiȝe þinges goode and blessed and digne. Þis vertue oure gret philosophre Ihesu Christ clepeþ perseueraunce wel lastynge, wher-bi þe goode Goddes knyȝtes suffreþ þe hardenesses and endureþ riȝt to þe end in þilke hiȝe weie of parfitnesse þat he haþ undertake."[4] Accordingly, Arthur's enterprise in its purpose has "grete hiȝenesse" and in its insistency of pursuit exhibits the ability to endure "riȝt to þe end in þilke hiȝe weie of parfitnesse þat he haþ undertake."

The height of Arthur's enterprise is impressed upon him in his dream in the manner of the wooing and the disclosure of the identity of the "royall Maid" who seeks his love.

> Was neuer hart so rauisht with delight,
> Ne liuing man like words did euer heare,
> As she to me deliuered all that night;
> And at her parting said, She Queene of Faeries hight.
>   [I.ix.14]

Arthur regards her favor as a high achievement in his conversation with Guyon, and Guyon assures him that it is both a high and a possible goal.

> Noble Lord, what meed so great,
> Or grace of earthly Prince so soueraine,
> But by your wondrous worth and warlike feat
> Ye well may hope, and easely attaine?
> But were your will, her sold to entertaine,
> And numbred be mongst knights of *Maydenhed,*
> Great guerdon, well I wote, should you remaine,
> And in her fauour high be reckoned.   [II.ix.6]

Chaucer's Parson defines the high achievement of magnificence as "whan a man dooth and perfourneth grete werkes of goodnesse," adding that "in the acomplissynge of grete goode werkes lith the grete gerdoun."[5] Although the "grete gerdoun" in the Parson's sermon is heavenly favor whereas the "great guerdon" of Gloriana is earthly honor, the moral character of the achievement is implicit in both Chaucer's and Spenser's versions of the concept. Arthur's vision of Gloriana is, in its allegorical import, a vision of the possibilities of moral perfection.

Just as the high enterprise of magnificence must begin in a true dream—in the contemplation of "hiȝe þinges goode and blessed and digne"—it may be subverted by a false. Arthur's dream is meant to contrast with the "fit false dreame" that causes Red Cross to swerve from his proper quest (I.i—ii) and the voluptuous reverie of Cymochles in the Bower of Bliss (II.v.28—34). All are products of enchantment and vehicles of seduction. But Arthur's alone is rooted in reality. The messenger from Archimago to Morpheus returns with the dream "by the Yuorie dore" (I.i.44), the gate of false dreams; similarly, the gate of the Bower of Bliss "framed was of precious yuory" (II.xii.44). Arthur's dream, in contrast, leaves behind an evidence of its substantiality: the "pressed gras, where she had lyen" (I.ix.15). Arthur's dream alone is capable, as well as worthy, of consummation.

Unlike the false dreams of Red Cross and Cymochles, Arthur's dream inspires a genuine and enduring love.

> From that day forth I lou'd that face diuine;
> From that day forth I cast in carefull mind,
> To seeke her out with labour, and long tyne,
> And neuer vow to rest, till her I find,
> Nine monethes I seeke in vaine yet ni'll that vow vnbind.
>
> [I.ix.15]

A high enterprise must be sustained by a deep and unremitting fidelity that permits no slackening of pace or deviation until the end is realized. This is the second quality of magnificence: "perseueraunce wel lastynge."

The opposite of high aspiration, in terms of the love metaphor, is lust, and of perseverance, sloth.[6] Arthur's antithesis, in these respects, is the Witch's Son,

A laesie loord, for nothing good to donne,
But stretched forth in idlenesse alwayes,
Ne euer cast his mind to couet prayse,
Or ply him selfe to any honest trade,
But all the day before the sunny rayes
He vs'd to slug, or sleepe in slothfull shade:
Such laesinesse both lewd and poor attonce him made.

{III.vii.12}

Smitten with the beauty of Florimell,

the Chorle through her so kind
And curteise vse conceiu'd affection bace,
And cast to loue her in his brutish mind;
No loue, but brutish lust, that was so beastly tind.

His lust, however, was unequal to the pursuit of "hiʒe þinges goode and blessed and digne."

Closely the wicked flame his bowels brent,
And shortly grew into outrageous fire;
Yet had he not the hart, nor hardiment,
As vnto her to vtter his desire;
His caytiue thought durst not so high aspire.

{III.vii.15–16}

The consequence of his forfeiting the true is his embracing of the false Florimell (III.viii.10). The churl's ability to accept a counterfeit and forget his pursuit of the true is an evidence of his deficiency in both high ambition and perseverance.

Spenser's description of Arthur's love and its consequences in his quest is a precise definition of the virtue he is said to represent in its two qualities of high ambition and perseverance:

Wonder it is to see, in diuerse minds,
How diuersly loue doth his pageants play,
And shewes his powre in variable kinds:
The baser wit, whose idle thoughts alway
Are wont to cleaue vnto the lowly clay,

> It stirreth vp to sensuall desire,
> And in lewd slouth to wast his carelesse day:
> But in braue sprite it kindles goodly fire,
> That to all high desert and honour doth aspire.
>
> Ne suffereth it vncomely idlenesse,
> In his free thought to build her sluggish nest:
> Ne suffereth it thought of vngentlenesse,
> Euer to creepe into his noble brest,
> But to the highest and the worthiest
> Lifteth it vp, that else would lowly fall:
> It lets not fall, it lets it not to rest:
> It lets not scarse this Prince to breath at all,
> But to his first poursuit him forward still doth call.
>
> [III.v. 1–2]

In his aspiration "to all high desert and honour" and his unrelenting "poursuit," Arthur exemplifies the virtue understood by medieval and Renaissance readers as magnificence.

As magnificence Arthur displays that steadiness of purpose and tenacity of application necessary to overcome the vices one by one and replace them with their opposing virtues. Arthur's perfection is a process of perfecting, and his cumulative acquisition of the virtues of the books is represented in his identification with the patron knights in their quests. Arthur's cleaving one of the heads of Duessa's purple beast (I.viii.16) anticipates Red Cross's splitting the scalp of the dragon (I.xi.35) as the first stroke of the bruising of the serpent's head that will fulfill the prophecy of Genesis 3:15. (The dragon eventually dies by a thrust through the mouth.) Arthur's use of Guyon's sword in the fight with the brothers Pyrochles and Cymochles, his accompanying Guyon to Alma's castle, and his battle against Maleger and his bands indicate his proficiency in temperance. The cumulative process is evident at the beginning of Book III, when, after tilting with Britomart, Guyon is placated by the Palmer and reconciled with the knight of chastity:

> In which accord the Prince was also plaste,
> And with that golden chaine of concord tyde.
> So goodly all agreed, they forth yfere did ryde. [III.i.12]

In Book IV Arthur, in addition to attacking and defeating embodiments of sensuality (enemies alike to chaste sexual love and the marriage of true minds that is friendship), performs a reconciling function. After rescuing Placidas from Corflambo, he restores him to his friend Amyas—along with Amyas's love, Aemylia—and reconciles Placidas to Paeana, daughter of Corflambo. Thereupon, Arthur, "whose minde did trauell as with chylde, / Of his old loue, conceau'd in secret brest, / Resolued to pursue his former quest" (IV.ix.17). Allegorically he is, in these interventions, remaining faithful to "his former quest" in demonstrating the virtues essential to the ideal of moral perfection that will secure the favor of Gloriana. His conquest of the vice represented by Corflambo is shown in his behavior toward Amoret while she remains in his company.

> But cause of feare sure had she none at all
> Of him, who goodly learned had of yore
> The course of loose affection to forstall,
> And lawlesse lust to rule with reasons lore;
> That all the while he by his side her bore,
> She was as safe as in a Sanctuary. [IV.ix.19]

Arthur has demonstrated rational control of loose affection in his defeat of Cymochles (II.viii) but exercises it in Book IV as a concomitant of friendship. Arthur has another opportunity to make peace after helping Britomart and Scudamour subdue their opponents Druon, Claribell, Blandamour, and Paridell. In Arthur's causing them to discuss their grievances, they recognize their common circumstances and come into accord with one another (IV.ix.20–41). In Book V Arthur is closely associated with Artegall from the time of his appearance in the narrative. In the rescue of Samient, Arthur slays one of her pursuers,

Artegall the other. Arthur and Artegall then tilt, but on recognizing one another embrace and vow "Neuer thenceforth to nourish enmity, / But either others cause to maintaine mutually" (viii.14). They go together to defeat the Soldan, Artegall in disguise as one of the slain knights and Arthur accompanied by Talus, Artegall's page. After overcoming the Soldan, who reigned "through lawlesse powre and tortious wrong," Arthur and Artegall capture Malengin, or Guyle. Having witnessed Mercilla's administration of justice to Duessa, Arthur and Artegall pursue separate but parallel missions against exemplars of tyrannous force and guile, Arthur's against Geryoneo and Artegall's against Grantorto. After liberating the kingdom of Belge, Arthur "to his former iourney him addrest, / On which long way he rode, ne euer day did rest" (xi.35). Arthur's "former iourney" brings him, in Book VI, to the aid of victims of discourtesy of a highly aggravated nature. He rescues Timias first from Decetto, Despetto, and Defetto (canto v) and later from the giant Disdain (canto viii). Arthur's defeat and baffling of Turpine, in revenge for his outrageous attack on the unarmed Calepine (cantos vi and vii), recalls Calidore's overthrowing of Crudor, instigator of Briana's shameful practice toward wayfaring knights and ladies (canto i). Both recreants are granted their lives at their request and in consideration of their ladies. Although Arthur never meets Calidore, he is identified with the knight of courtesy in the similarity of his foes and of the circumstances of his provocation and combat.

Arthur's intervention in the affairs of the patron knights accords with Spenser's statement in the Letter to Raleigh relating Arthur's adventures to the separate books: "In the whole course I mention the deedes of Arthure applyable to that vertue, which I write of in that booke." Arthur's quest comprises the quests of the other knights and cannot end until they have completed their missions.[7] Arthur's resuming his quest after each intervention signifies his having demonstrated his proficiency in the particular virtue of the book and the assimilation of that virtue to the moral ideal of magnificence.

In its double nature, magnificence is also the virtue that the reader requires if he is to complete his quest. It takes both high ambition and perseverance to follow Arthur, virtue by virtue, through Fairyland, sharing his quest in order to partake of his reward: the favor of the great queen. If the reader continues, however, he will have enabled the poet to have fulfilled (to the extent of the poem's existing limits) his twofold purpose: "to fashion a gentleman or noble person in vertuous and gentle discipline." For the fashioning of Arthur, book by book, is the fashioning of the reader. Since the fashioning will require twelve books, the urgency of the reader's exercise of magnificence is periodically enforced by hortatory pointing. He needs both height and steadiness of purpose:

> Young knight, what euer that dost armes professe,
> And through long labours huntest after fame,
> Beware of fraud, beware of ficklenesse,
> In choice, and change of thy deare loued Dame,
> Least thou of her beleeue too lightly blame,
> And rash misweening doe thy hart remoue:
> For vnto knight there is no greater shame,
> Then lightnesse and inconstancie in loue.   [I.iv.1]

He needs perseverance, concerning which Spenser has Guyon admonish Arthur, glancing at the reader: "But you faire Sir, be not herewith dismaid, / But constant keepe the way, in which ye stand" (II.ix.8). The reader is often spurred by examples of wasted possibilities. Of Phedon, the Palmer moralizes,

>   Most wretched man,
>   That to affections does the bridle lend;
>   In their beginning they are weake and wan,
>   But soone through suff'rance grow to fearefull end.
>   [II.iv.34]

The cases of Trevisan, Mordant, and Verdant—all winsome but careless young knights—speak eloquently of the tragedy of the impaired quest. Concerning Archimago, that grand subverter of magnificence, Spenser warns,

> For all he did, was to deceiue good knights,
> And draw them from pursuit of praise and fame,
> To slug in slouth and sensuall delights,
> And end their daies with irrenowmed shame. [II.i.23]

The acknowledgment by the narrator of a long and tedious journey, though delightful, is a tutor's encouragement of his pupil to persevere in his quest. The ends of the books are only temporary resting places:

> Now strike your sailes ye iolly Mariners,
> For we be come vnto a quiet rode,
> Where we must land some of our passengers,
> And light this wearie vessell of her lode.
> Here she a while may make her safe abode,
> Till she repaired haue her tackles spent,
> And wants supplide. And then againe abroad
> On the long voyage whereto she is bent:
> Well may she speede and fairely finish her intent. [I.xii.42]

Upon the completion by the reader (to be sure, an ideal reader) of the long voyage or quest or journey (VI.Pro. 1—2), Fairyland will have nurtured two exemplars of magnificence. Magnificence will have been demonstrated by the reader, as well as by Arthur, both in the process of the quest and in the perfection of the finished pattern. Spenser will have fulfilled not only his own stated purpose in the Letter to Raleigh but also the aim of the epic poet according to Sidney in having bestowed a hero upon the world. The ideal will have become fused with the real, and Arthur will have returned to England.

2 · *The Garden of Virtue*

The centrality of moral nurture in *The Faerie Queene* is evident in the prevalence of the idea of fostering. The poem continually impresses upon the reader the effects of nurture on the formation of character. Satyrane, "noursled vp in life and manners wilde," is limited by his education, having learned only "To banish cowardize and bastard feare" (I.vi.23–24). Braggadocchio's inept handling of Guyon's steed made it plain to all that "He had not trayned bene in cheualree" (II.iii.46). Britomart, in her conversation with Red Cross, attributes her martial manner to her upbringing, rather than to her natural inclination:

> Faire Sir, I let you weete, that from the howre
> I taken was from nourses tender pap,
> I haue beene trained vp in warlike stowre,
> To tossen speare and shield, and to affrap
> The warlike ryder to his most mishap;
> Sithence I loathed haue my life to lead,
> As Ladies wont, in pleasures wanton lap,
> To finger the fine needle and nyce thread;
> Me leuer were with point of foemans speare be dead.
>
> [III.ii.6]

The irony that her fostering has, after all, been ineffectual, as was Marinell's (III.iv.20), in submerging her sexual nature still does not minimize the force of nurture in carrying the individual so far against his grain. The potency of fostering is emphasized in Calepine's words to Matilda:

> Lo how good fortune doth to you present
> This litle babe, of sweete and louely face,
> And spotlesse spirit, in which ye may enchace
> What euer formes ye list thereto apply,

> Being now soft and fit them to embrace;
> Whether ye list him traine in cheualry,
> Or noursle vp in lore in learn'd Philosophy.   [VI.iv.35]

The newly born twins Belphoebe and Amoret are discovered by Venus and Diana and carried away "to be fostered" in such a fashion as to produce characters consistent with their manner of conception and indicated in their names (III.vi.28). In *The Faerie Queene* the definition of character commonly consists of the identification of parentage or lineage; a description of the upbringing, including method and place; and the conferring of an appropriate name. When nature, nurture, and name conjoin, the result is especially potent for good. It is also, however, potent for evil. Spenser, emphasizing the viciousness of the Blatant Beast, gives him a fitting nature, nurture, and name.

> It is a Monster bred of hellishe race,
> . . . .
> Of *Cerberus* whilome he was begot,
> And fell *Chimaera* in her darkesome den,
> Through fowle commixture of his filthy blot;
> Where he was fostred long in *Stygian* fen,
> Till he to perfect ripenesse grew, and then
> Into this wicked world he forth was sent,
> To be the plague and scourge of wretched men:
> Whom with vile tongue and venemous intent
> He sore doth wound, and bite, and cruelly torment.
>   [VI.i.7–8]

The name may be a prophecy of the kind of character that will be produced or a record of the kind of character that has been produced by the joint intentions of nature and nurture, and "perfect ripenesse" suggests the readiness of the individual to live up to his name.

The place of nurture in the cases of Belphoebe, Amoret, and the Blatant Beast, as well as generally in *The Faerie*

Queene, is apart from the world of ordinary life. The nurture, as a rule, is under the supervision of a foster parent. The babe Pastorella, destined to be an exemplar of natural courtesy, was discovered abandoned in the fields by Meliboe and committed to the care of his wife, "Who as her owne it nurst, and named euermore" (VI.xii.9). Artegall was removed by Astraea from "Amongst his peres playing his childish sport" to a cave, "In which she noursled him, till yeares he raught, / And all the discipline of iustice there him taught" (v.i.6). Secluded from the world of mankind under the tutelage of Astraea, he practices justice on the wild beasts "Vntill the ripenesse of mans yeares he raught" (v.i.8). Then, armed with Jove's sword and attended by Talus, Artegall goes into the world to exercise the skills in which he has been trained. Evidently nurture requires withdrawal into a carefully designed artificial environment—a nursery—from which one may return with the knowledge and skills and the moral qualities essential to success in his sphere of responsibility.

Artegall's fostering, like his name, evokes that of Arthur, the most notable foster child in *The Faerie Queene.* In Arthur's, as in Artegall's, upbringing there is separation from natural parents, intensive education in precepts, arming, and a quest in Fairyland that is a prelude to the enactment of the role for which he has been fitted by birth, name, and education. The reader's is a similar case. The poet, as a wise foster parent, is collaborating with those responsible for the formal education of his charge in bestowing on him a character becoming to his nobility of birth. The artificial environment—the nursery—is the poem. The realm of the poem is for the reader what Fairyland is for the other knights who journey toward Cleopolis.

The knights of Fairyland are carefully distinguished as natives of Fairyland or human visitors. The human knights are youths of noble birth who have been brought to Fairyland in infancy or have come on a quest. During their sojourn in Fairyland they receive certain instruction and undertake certain missions that will prepare them for their later careers. Sir Tristram, for example, is a youth of seventeen, son of a Cornish king, who has been sent to Fairyland for protection from his uncle. During his seven-year visit he has grown "to stature strong" and made good use of his time:

> All which my daies I haue not lewdly spent,
> Nor spilt the blossome of my tender yeares
> In ydlesse, but as was conuenient,
> Haue trayned bene with many noble feres
> In gentle thewes, and such like seemely leres. [VI.ii.31]

His education, however, has omitted the arts of combat, and to remedy this deficiency Tristram urges Calidore to accept him as his squire. Calidore, "For the rare hope which in his yeares appear'd," undertakes his education in arms, whereupon

> Full glad and ioyous then young *Tristram* grew,
> Like as a flowre, whose silken leaues small,
> Long shut vp in the bud from heauens vew,
> At length breakes forth, and brode displayes his smyling
>   hew.   [VI.ii.35]

The account emphasizes potentialities. Tristram's natural gifts can be brought to fruition (the bud and flower image is significant of development) only by the proper education, which is now overdue. Tristram's education will take the form of the emulation of Calidore's example. The exact nature of Tristram's future role is not revealed in the existing portion of the poem, but his royal lineage indicates that it will not be an insignificant one.

Red Cross and Artegall are brought in infancy to Fairyland, whereas Britomart comes on a quest for her lover.[1] Arthur's history combines these circumstances. Immediately after birth,

From mothers pap I taken was vnfit:
And streight deliuered to a Faery knight,
To be vpbrought in gentle thewes and martiall might.

                                                              [I.ix.3]

Committed by Merlin to the tutelage of Timon, Arthur remained ignorant of his lineage and destiny except that he was "sonne and heire vnto a king" (I.ix.5). One day, "in freshest flowre of youthly yeares, / When courage first does creepe in manly chest" (I.ix.9), he dreamed that he was wooed by the Fairy Queen, "with whose excellent beauty rauished, he awaking resolued to seeke her out, and so being by Merlin armed, and by Timon throughly instructed, he went to seek her forth in Faerye land" (Letter to Raleigh). Having arrived at Fairyland by fairy sleight and by personal volition, Arthur pursues a quest that will culminate in his reign as emperor of Britain. Fictionally he has finished his education "in vertuous lore"; allegorically his preparation continues as he participates in the quests of the other knights. Likewise the reader, having arrived in the fictional world of the poem by the allurement of cunning artifice or by deliberate choice, pursues a quest for the qualities that will win him the favor of his queen and fit him for a responsible role in the service of England.

The allegorical meaning of Fairyland is disclosed in the poet's reply to the downright empiricist in the Proem to Book II. The recent discoveries of Peru, the Amazon River, and Virginia warrant belief in the existence of undiscovered lands. Perhaps other worlds exist "within the Moones faire shining spheare" and in other heavenly bodies. "Why then should witlesse man so much misweene / That nothing is, but that which he hath seene?" After hinting at his meaning "By certaine signes here set in sundry place"—namely, the Amazon, Virginia, and the moon (Cynthia)—Spenser spells it out in direct address to the Queen:

And thou, O fairest Princesse vnder sky,
In this faire mirrhour maist behold thy face,

And thine owne realmes in lond of Faery,
And in this antique Image thy great auncestry.   [4]

Fairyland is a mirror in the twofold Elizabethan sense of a reflecting surface and an exemplar. As a reflection, Fairyland is a compliment to Elizabeth and her kingdom. As an exemplar, Fairyland is a prophetic ideal.[2] It images the promise of England, which will become reality when her citizens and courtiers accept the challenge and submit to the influence of this heroic poem. "But yet the end is not," Merlin exclaims at the close of his prophetic utterance (III.iii.50). Fairyland is at once a compliment to the real and a hortatory prophecy of the ideal.

As a reflection of the real and an embodiment of the ideal, Fairyland presents a threefold image: of Elizabeth's person, realms, and ancestry (st. 4).[3] It has thus a personal, spatial, and temporal aspect. In its personal aspect Fairyland presents examples of Elizabeth's virtues and their expression in her administration of England's affairs. In the Letter to Raleigh and in the Proem to Book III, Spenser alerts the reader to the images of Elizabeth in Gloriana and Belphoebe, who represent her private and political persons. In Mercilla Elizabeth is shown suppressing her natural inclination to show mercy in deference to the good of her kingdom. Reflections of Elizabeth's person appear in Una and elsewhere. But in a larger sense Elizabeth's glory illumines all of Fairyland. The radiance of her imputed moral perfection informs the concept of Gloriana and her court. It inspires the quests of the Knights of Maidenhead and rewards their triumphs, which are a part of her fame and contribute to the health of her kingdom. The splendor of the virtues of Gloriana and her court is not only a personal compliment to Elizabeth but also the ideal toward which all must strive who would gain her favor. The reader, like Arthur, strives through moral combat to win her approval and add to her glory.

Spatially, Fairyland has been regarded as the world of

Spenser's fiction and as the otherworld within Spenser's
fiction. In its stricter geographical sense it is neither of these
but rather the dominion of the Fairy Queen. Beyond Fairyland, by this definition, lie the realms of Belge and Irena.
Distinct from it are the regions of Wales and Cornwall (in
earlier times known as West Wales), the less civilized
southwest corners of England from which the Briton
knights enter the land of Fairy. (Arthur and Britomart enter
from South Wales; Artegall is brought from Cornwall; Sir
Tristram is sent from Lyonesse, a legendary island or penin-
sula west of Land's End. Red Cross, a Saxon, enters from
an undisclosed location.) To the north are the territories of
the "Lord of *Many Ilands*" and the "Prince of *Picteland*"
(VI.xii.4). At its center is Cleopolis, a London that recapitulates and surpasses the glories of the ancient imperial seats of
Troy and Rome as their lineal successor (II.x.72–73).[4]
Fairyland proper is the main sphere of its civilizing
influence, an ideal England bounded in the Elizabethan
imagination by the Tamar, the Severn, and the Tweed.[5]

A. L. Rowse has recounted the concerned attempts and
gradually succeeding effort of the Tudor monarchs to subdue and integrate into English society the borderlands to
the west and the north that remained as vestiges of a
primitive Celtic society.[6] Spenser's own administrative
duties must have sharpened his awareness of the cultural
disparity between England and its outlying territories and
his sense of the importance of expanding its social frontiers.
The title by which Spenser addresses Sir Walter Raleigh in
the prefatory letter—"Lo. Wardein of the Stanneryes [the
courts for the tin miners in Cornwall and Devonshire] and
her Maiesties liefetenaunt of the County of Corne-
waylle"—points up Raleigh's role in the civilization of the
western lands, a role that included not only his jurisdiction
in Devonshire and Cornwall and his estate-holding in Ireland but also his colonization of the New World. Raleigh's
civilizing role must have made his support of Spenser's own

civilizing effort in *The Faerie Queene* seem, to Spenser, especially appropriate. Clearly it is a conviction of the possibility
of a united, civilized England, still socially fragmented into
the regions inherited by Brutus's three sons (II.x. 13–14),
that underlies Spenser's spatial definition of Fairyland and
gives special point and sublimity to such an image as the
marriage of the rivers in Book IV.

In the case of Wales, however, there existed among
Spenser's readers and in Spenser himself an ambivalency of
feeling; for, despite its backwardness, from it had emerged,
or reemerged, the promise of England. In Merlin's prophetic account of English history onward from Arthur, the
Britons, "for their sinnes dew punishment," are to be
subdued by the Saxons and "Banisht from Princely bowre to
wastfull wood." ("Princely bowre" refers not only to luxuri-
ous living but also to England as, in the words of Shakespeare's John of Gaunt, a "nurse," a "teeming womb of royal
kings.") After "twise foure hundreth yeares," they will
return from their wilderness of exile and resume their rule
(III.iii.41–42,44). With the accession of the unapologeti-
cally Welsh Henry VII, Wales secured a new status in the
national consciousness. Numerous Welshmen trooped to
London in Henry's train to settle and acquire positions of
influence, among them David Cecil, grandfather of Lord
Burghley, from an obscure border family. In fact, as well as
in the still fashionable and officially credited Tudor myth,
Wales had distinguished itself as a region of rich potentialities.

In the moral allegory, Wales (inclusive of Cornwall) is to
Fairyland, and particularly to its capital city, as unnurtured
nature is to a fully civilized character. Arthur's quest, beginning in Wales and ending in Cleopolis, allegorically
implies the reader's education. The reader, like Arthur,
must set out from Wales for Cleopolis. To arrive there, he
must submit himself, virtue by virtue, to the disciplining
influence of Gloriana and her court that emanates from her

imperial city and pervades Fairyland. In the reader's education, as in Arthur's quest, the potentialities inherent in high birth and the native stock are cultivated and refined in anticipation of the time when the resulting qualities of character will be recognized and given scope for their exercise in a position of responsibility, influence, and fame. The moral action of the poem in terms of the geographical symbolism is the extension of the civilizing influence of Cleopolis over the back country, the reclamation of the "wastfull wood" from which the hope of England has emerged. The geography of Fairyland thus symbolically reinforces its function as both the agency and goal of the moral perfection of the reader.[7]

In its temporal aspect Fairyland is antiquity. It provides an "antique Image" in which Elizabeth may behold her "great auncestry" (II.Pro.4). The representation of the Tudor myth in the Briton genealogy (from Brut to Arthur in the Briton Chronicle, II.x.1−68, and from Arthur to Elizabeth in Merlin's prophecy, III.iii.26−50) is part of the poem's homage to Elizabeth. Whereas the Briton Chronicle includes the sordid realities of English history along with the sublime, the Elfin Chronicle (II.x.70−76) displays the glories of recent English history in an idealized account of England under the Tudors as the lineal successor and surpasser of the great civilizations of the past (Rathborne, pp. 126−28). As both the "royall virgin" of Briton descent and the Gloriana-Tanaquill of fairy descent, Elizabeth represents the restoration of the legitimate Briton line and the temporal consummation of the timeless fairy dynasty in a union of the real and ideal.

But the reflection of Elizabeth's "great auncestry" in the "antique Image" of Fairyland is more comprehensive than the content of the genealogies. It is necessary at this point to qualify the simple equation of Fairyland and antiquity. Antiquity, for Spenser, provides a standard of virtue by which later times can be measured and, if necessary, condemned. The festive board of the King and Queen of Eden was

> but bare and plaine:
> For th'antique world excesse and pride did hate;
> Such proud luxurious pompe is swollen vp but late.
>
> [I.xii.14]

The use of the Golden Age myth, whether satirical or merely nostalgic, was an old and well-worn device of poets (*Variorum*, 5:156). Yet it amounts to something more fundamental in *The Faerie Queene* than decorative convention. The fullest statements of the myth in the poem are in Book IV, canto viii, and in the Proem to Book V. In these passages Spenser praises the innocence of the first age, when

> The Lyon there did with the Lambe consort,
> And eke the Doue sate by the Faulcons side,
> Ne each of other feared fraud or tort,
> But did in safe securitie abide,
> Withouten perill of the stronger pride.   [IV.viii.31]

But when the world grew old, good began to be overthrown and perverted by evil (IV.viii.32). It is necessary therefore for the poet to form his exemplars of virtue on the pattern of antiquity.

> Let none then blame me, if in discipline
> Of vertue and of ciuill vses lore,
> I doe not forme them to the common line
> Of present dayes, which are corrupted sore,
> But to the antique vse, which was of yore,
> When good was onely for it selfe desyred,
> And all men sought their owne, and none no more;
> When Iustice was not for most meed outhyred,
> But simple Truth did rayne, and was of all admyred.
>
> [V.Pro.3]

Yet Fairyland cannot be equated with the age of primal innocence. Eden is under siege. Saturn has been banished by Jove. The Titans, though overthrown, have left their offspring to trouble the world. Astraea has fled. The friends of virtue daily do battle with the practicers of force and fraud. In the kingdom of Gloriana, Archimago is at large; Ate is busy; and the Blatant Beast is on the ramp. Rather, in Fairyland the goodness of antiquity is arrayed against the powers responsible for the deterioration of the later ages. (Guyon, for example, disputing with Mammon, assigns the material values with which he is being tempted to "later ages pride," ii.vii.16.) In the realization of the ideal of Cleopolis in the rule of Elizabeth

> Sprung of the auncient stocke of Princes straine,
> Now th'onely remnant of that royall breed,
> Whose noble kind at first was sure of heauenly seed
>
> [iv.viii.33]

there is a reassertion of the principles of antiquity in the re-creation of the ancient order. Elizabeth's reign is the result of a providential conjunction of earthly virtue and power that enables the degeneration to be arrested and the frontiers of moral chaos and social barbarity to be thrown back to the ancient lines. Fairyland presents not the Golden Age but an image of ancient virtues combating present evils. Elizabeth, as Gloriana, is a perfect embodiment of these ancient virtues, and her "great auncestry" is, therefore, all the types of virtue active in Fairyland.

As an educational treatise, *The Faerie Queene* is typical of Renaissance humanism in recommending the pursuit of an education in antiquity. But the antiquity of Fairyland is obviously not the antiquity of the historian. It is the antiquity of the poet, who may improve on the inconsistency of history in showing vice punished and virtue rewarded and, moreover, in the creation of an exemplar. As the "antique Image" has been restored in Elizabeth's reign—to the extent Fairyland is recognizable as England—so in the reader the virtues of the great exemplars of old, compacted in Arthur, may once again engage the powers of evil. In fact

the full realization of the "antique Image" in Elizabethan
England depends upon the tractability of all the human
visitors lured by the spell of heroic poetry into Fairyland.

The idea of the nursery of virtue affects not only the spatial
and temporal setting but also the arrangement of the virtues
themselves. In the Proem to Book VI the poet requests of
the muses,

> Reuele to me the sacred noursery
> Of vertue, which with you doth there remaine,
> Where it in siluer bowre does hidden ly
> From view of men, and wicked worlds disdaine.
> Since it at first was by the Gods with paine
> Planted in earth, being deriu'd at furst
> From heauenly seedes of bounty soueraine,
> And by them long with carefull labour nurst,
> Till it to ripenesse grew, and forth to honour burst.   [3]

In this secluded place the virtues grow as plants. Courtesy,
for example, is a flower "Which though it on a lowly stalke
doe bowre, / Yet brancheth forth in braue nobilitie, / And
spreds it selfe through all ciuilitie" (st. 4). The description
of chastity, another flower in the nursery of virtue, distinguishes the earthly nursery from a heavenly archetype.

> Eternall God in his almighty powre,
> To make ensample of his heauenly grace,
> In Paradize whilome did plant this flowre;
> Whence he it fetcht out of her natiue place,
> And did in stocke of earthly flesh enrace,
> That mortall men her glory should admire:
> In gentle Ladies brest, and bounteous race
> Of woman kind it fairest flowre doth spire,
> And beareth fruit of honour and all chast desire. [III.v.52]

The virtues that grow natively in paradise have been trans-
planted into earthly nurseries and left under the custody of
the muses. These nurseries are the minds of men and women

who are receptive to the implantation of the heavenly seeds and the cultivation of them by the muses. The virtues have been implanted from birth within the natives of Fairyland: in Belphoebe, described above, and in Calidore, "In whom it seemes, that gentlenesse of spright / And manners mylde were planted naturall" (VI.i.2). Spenser's readers, however, must with the help of the muses nourish these virtues themselves by following good examples and shunning evil examples:

> Faire Ladies, that to loue captiued arre,
> And chaste desires do nourish in your mind,
> Let not her [Malecasta's] fault your sweet affections marre,
> Ne blot the bounty of all womankind;
> 'Mongst thousands good one wanton Dame to find.
>
> [III.i.49]

Secluded "From view of men, and wicked worlds disdaine" in their nursery "deepe within the mynd," the virtues are cultivated to ripeness (VI.Pro.3,5).

The custody of the muses over the nursery of virtue is an expression of the importance of poetry in moral education. It assumes the instrumentality of Calliope, as well as of the patronesses of the academic arts, in bringing the virtues to fruition. Sidney places the poet, as a cultivator of virtue, above the philosopher and historian, and the three of them above the lawyer, who is "not in the deepest trueth to stande in rancke with these who all indeuour to take naughtines away, and plant goodnesse euen in the secretest cabinet of our soules" (1:164). Una remarks to Arthur after hearing his account of his vision of Gloriana, "True Loues are often sown, but seldom grow on ground" (I.ix.16). Poetry excels all other arts in inculcating "True Loues"—worthy aspirations—till they grow to ripeness and "forth to honour burst." [8] The answer of the muses to their invocation by the poet in the Proem to Book VI is a revelation of the supreme pattern of all earthly nurseries of virtue: the mind of Elizabeth (st. 6).

The notion of the garden of virtues in the mind derives from a long tradition of medieval and patristic biblical exegesis beginning with Philo Judaeus. In *Noah's Work as a Planter* Philo asks what plants God planted in the Garden. They could not have been actual trees, he assumes, for God could have no need of the fruits of such plants. Since "trees of Life, of Immortality, of Knowledge, of Apprehension, of Understanding, of the conception of good and evil . . . can be no growths of earthly soil, but must be those of the reasonable soul . . . we must conceive therefore that the bountiful God plants in the soul as it were a garden of virtues and of the modes of conduct corresponding to each of them, a garden that brings the soul to perfect happiness."[9] This garden described in Genesis 2 is "a copy of the heavenly and archetypal excellence" where the virtues grow natively in the presence of God. The Tree of Life is "virtue in the most comprehensive sense, which some term goodness." The four rivers in Eden are the four cardinal virtues.[10] Adam's responsibility to dress the garden Philo interprets as "soul-husbandry": "Who else could the man that is in each of us be save the mind, whose place it is to reap the benefits derived from all that has been sown or planted? But seeing that for babes milk is food, but for grown men wheaten bread, there must also be soul-nourishment, such as is milk-like suited to the time of childhood, in the shape of instructions leading the way through wisdom and temperance and all virtue. For these when sown and planted in the mind will produce most beneficial fruits, namely fair and praiseworthy conduct." Soul-husbandry in childhood includes "the whole of the education embraced in school-learning." For older youths Philo prescribes "the plant of sound sense, that of courage, that of temperance, that of justice, that of all virtue."[11] It is interesting that the education in the cardinal virtues and "all virtue" is appropriate after the formal education in the academic subjects. Its place seems to correspond to that of the agency of poetry in the "vertuous and gentle discipline" envisaged by Spenser.

Philo's commentary on Genesis was well known in the Renaissance.[12] His allegorical interpretation of the Garden of Eden was also inherited through the writings of the church fathers and of the medieval churchmen. After Augustine's interpretation of Genesis 2:15 as enjoining the husbandry of the soul, the allegorical and literal interpretations vied in patristic and medieval exegesis of the passage.[13] In Ambrose's homily *De Paradiso* paradise is "a land of fertility—that is to say, a soul which is fertile—planted in Eden, that is, in a certain delightful or well-tilled land in which the soul finds pleasure. Adam exists there as *nous* [mind] and Eve as 'sense.'" The stream that rises from paradise and branches into four streams is wisdom. It "rises from the soul when well tilled, not from the soul which lies uncultivated. The results therefrom are fruit trees of diverse virtues. There are four principal virtues: prudence, temperance, fortitude, and justice."[14]

The garden of virtue in the mind is prominent in both learned theological and popular devotional discussions of the virtues in the later medieval period. It is also common in Renaissance writings more ethical than specifically religious in purpose. It is expounded at tedious length in Barnabe Googe's translation of Palingenius's *The Zodiake of Life*.

And first, as nature so disposing it the rude and Countrie
    fielde,
Except it oftentimes be tild, and eke with labour sore,
The hurtfull weedes with plough and rakes be causd to grow
    no more
Nor this enoughe, it needefull is good seedes therein to cast,
And dayly for to husband it till daunger all be past.
Euen so the minde whilst it is bounde within the body here,
Is ouergrowne with Briers sharp, and wilde it doth appeare:

Except it ayded be with helpe of one that tilleth well,
And aptly vertues therin plantes, and vices doth expell.

Iago applies the concept to the power of the will to control
the impulses of the body: "Virtue! a fig! 'tis in ourselves that
we are thus or thus. Our bodies are our gardens, to the
which our wills are gardeners; so that if we will plant nettles
or sow lettuce, set hyssop and weed up thyme, supply it
with one gender of herbs or distract it with many, either to
have it sterile with idleness or manured with industry, why,
the power and corrigible authority of this lies in our wills."
The garden of virtues could serve as a vehicle of pietism,
moralism, or egoism, depending on the agency of its cultivation. It had obvious potentialities as a structural image for
a Renaissance poem concerned with the moral culture of
youth.[15]

In another tradition of interpretation, paradise is a place
of instruction. Origen, commenting on Paul's visiting of
paradise (2 Cor. 12:2–4), concludes: "I think, therefore,
that all the saints who depart from this life will remain in
some place situated on the earth, which holy Scripture calls
paradise, as in some place of instruction, and, so to speak,
class-room or school of souls, in which they are to be
instructed regarding all the things which they had seen on
earth, and are to receive also some instruction respecting
things that are to follow in the future, as even when in this
life, they had obtained in some degree indications of future
events, although 'through a glass darkly,' all of which are
revealed more clearly and distinctly to the saints in their
proper time and place."[16] The allegorical garden of
medieval writers commonly offers a paradise for the instruction of the reader. Combining elements as diverse as the
classical *locus amoenus*, platonic and neoplatonic mythology,
and the Song of Songs, the garden embodies truths attainable only by the properly prepared and motivated mind and
shields them from the casual, profane curiosity. Both con-

cepts of the garden—as a planting of virtues in the mind and a place of instruction—appear in the celestial paradise of Alanus de Insulis. In the *Anticlaudianus,* when Phronesis, or Wisdom, ascends to the supreme palaces of the eternal King, she sees a brilliant fountain illumined by a sun that "subdues the sun in splendor." Alanus, describing its properties, explains that "the mind touched by this heat sprouts forth in flowers, and this heat beautifies the soil of the mind with the blessed blossom of virtues, while it leads back celestial spring." Nature cannot provide a remedy for the vices of the age. Only Wisdom, emanating from the heavenly courts of the Creator, can enable the virtues to "locate their abodes upon earth, and come into their kingdoms, and rule the world" by flourishing in the minds of men.[17] Alanus's garden is not only a phenomenon of the mind (with its heavenly archetype) but also a place for the reader's education in truths transcending the earthly. The enlightenment of Phronesis is the enlightenment of the reader.

We have, then, a firm basis in exegetical tradition, as well as in Spenser's own references to the flowers of chastity and courtesy and their bower, for regarding *The Faerie Queene* itself as a garden of virtue in both allegorical senses: a pattern to be cultivated in the reader's mind and a paradise, like the gardens of ancient Athens, for the instruction of the reader in moral philosophy. The "darke conceite" of the poem, like the "sacred noursery / Of vertue" described in the Proem to Book VI, "does hidden ly / From view of men and wicked worlds disdaine" (st. 3). Sixteenth-century readers were admitted to Spenser's great nursery of virtue in two installments, the editions of 1590 (Books I–III) and 1596 (Books I–VI). It is unlikely that they were surprised by the series of virtues they encountered or the manner of their arrangement.

In the Letter to Raleigh, Spenser proposes to treat "the twelue priuate morall vertues, as Aristotle hath deuised."

The correspondence of Spenser's specific six and his projected total of twelve to Aristotle's set of virtues in the *Ethics* has been warmly debated by Jusserand, De Moss, Winstanley, Hulbert, and others (*Variorum*, 1:327–30, 340–43, 353–57), and the attempt to correlate Spenser's and Aristotle's virtues has generally been judged unsuccessful (*Variorum* editors, 1:342–43; Renwick, *Variorum*, 1:361).[18] Josephine Bennett has stressed the importance to Spenser of a tradition of the virtues that competes with the *Ethics* in medieval and Renaissance moral treatises. This importance "can hardly be over emphasized." Bennett hypothesizes an original four-book scheme on the cardinal virtues that was later adapted to a twelve-book "Aristotelian" scheme (*Evolution*, pp. 229–30). Rosamund Tuve in the second chapter of *Allegorical Imagery* also emphasizes the importance of the cardinal virtues in Spenser's thought but without seeing their full implications for the framework of *The Faerie Queene*. In discussing the problem of the sources of Spenser's virtues, Tuve points out that there were three main sources of medieval treatments of the cardinal virtues: the sixth-century pseudo-Senecan *Formula honestae vitae* of Martin of Braga; Cicero's *De inventione* (ii.53–54); and Macrobius's *In somnium Scipionis* (i.viii). These authors "it would surely be ill-advised to excise from Spenser's claimed body of authorities, '*Aristotle and the rest*'" (p. 66). In the writings of each, the cardinal virtue appears in the company of other virtues that are related to it as its "aspects" or manifestations in particular situations. Medieval writers tended to be eclectic in supplementing their main source with additional virtues and definitions from other sources. Generally the ground plan was Macrobius's list, which "seems to have been universally used" (p. 63). Since Macrobius offered no definitions—only a list of the cardinal virtues and their related virtues—the nature of his influence was mainly structural.

Over a hundred years ago Thomas Keightley suggested

that it was perhaps Spenser's intention to use the cardinal virtues as the cores of his remaining three-book groupings, as he had done in Books II and V of the first two installments.[19] It is interesting that among the virtues associated by Macrobius with temperance are *castitas* and *pudicitia* (translated "purity" by Stahl), the virtues of Books III and I. Among those associated with justice are *amicitia* and *concordia,* the concerns of Book IV, and *humanitas,* for which Elyot's dictionary includes among its meanings "gentylnesse, meekenesse, curteysie, gentyll behauiour, ciuilitie, pleasauntnesse in manners," the concerns of Book VI.[20] *Constantia,* the virtue suggested by Spenser's 1609 editor as the theme of the book (VII?) for which the *Cantos of Mutabilitie* were intended, is associated by Macrobius with fortitude, which, it is tempting to conjecture, was the virtue designated for Book VIII. At any rate, the arrangement of the virtues in the six books published conforms clearly to the most influential medieval classification of the virtues.[21]

One of the most frequently encountered medieval pictorial devices for representing schematically the central virtues and their parts is that of a tree and its branches. A familiar example is its use by Chaucer's Parson in his sermon on penance. Spenser's friend Lodowyck Bryskett uses it structurally in his discussion of the cardinal virtues and their related virtues: "There are then by the generall consent of all men foure principall vertues appertaining to ciuill life, which are, Fortitude, Temperance, Iustice, and Prudence; from which foure are also deriued (as branches frō their trees) sundry others to make vp the number of twelue."[22] Bryskett's arrangement of the twelve virtues as four central virtues and their branches is strikingly similar to (though his specific list does not agree with) what we can see of Spenser's scheme. Spenser's positioning of the cardinal virtues between their branches in each grouping of three books permits the ancient contours of the garden of virtues to be

shadowed in the frame of his poem. His very arrangement of
the virtues creates a great Renaissance image of a medieval
commonplace and, in so doing, symbolizes the action of the
poem upon the reader's mind.

The garden of virtue is both the pattern of moral perfection
and the means of its achievement. As the mind of Gloriana,
it is the goal of both Arthur and the reader; for the quest for
Gloriana is the quest for the virtues of the great Queen and
their attendant honor. As the scene of this quest, it provides
the reader with a temporary residence in a secluded, artificial environment for fostering in "vertuous and gentle
discipline." Pliny recommends the use of nurseries for a
phase in the development of young plants: "All of these
[kinds of seedlings] it is customary not to put in their own
ground at once, but first to give them to a foster-mother and
let them grow up in seed-plots, and then change their
habitation again, this removal having a marvellously civilizing effect even on wild trees." [23] Evidently Spenser agreed
with Pliny that there is something about the transplanting
of scions into and from a proper nursery that helps to refine
their powers and fit them for a fruitful maturity.

PART II

A PRINCIPLE OF PROGRESSION: PUBLIC VIRTUE

And man hauing all these vertuous habits in
him . . . he hath also need of the conuersation
of other men, lest the occasiõ of doing vertu-
ously shold faile him. For though a mã haue
neuer so perfect a knowledge of al the vertues,
vnless he put them in action, he can neuer be
happie.

Lodowyck Bryskett, *A Discourse of Ciuill Life*

3 · *Active Virtue*

The direction of Arthur's quest—toward Cleopolis—is a part of the larger pattern projected for the twenty-four books of *The Faerie Queene* and its sequel. According to the Letter to Raleigh, the first twelve books were to treat the "twelue priuate morall vertues, as Aristotle hath deuised," and the second twelve, the political virtues. The completed scheme would present two poems, or halves of a poem, coextensive in their moral scope with the *Iliad* and *Odyssey* of Homer, "who in the Persons of Agamemnon and Vlysses hath ensampled a good gouernour and a vertuous man," and with the *Aeneid* of Virgil, who had combined these moral ideals in the example of Aeneas. It would also conform to the practice of Ariosto, who had combined the private and political virtues in Orlando, and of Tasso, who had distinguished them in Rinaldo and Godfredo. In Spenser's hero Arthur, as in Aeneas and Orlando, the private and political virtues would appear in combination. In the two parts of Arthur's career—as in the *Iliad* and the *Odyssey* and in the careers of Rinaldo and Godfredo—the private and political virtues would appear separately.

The distinction of private and political virtue was the traditional and still standard division of moral philosophy into ethics and politics according to the titles of Aristotle's works. This division of moral philosophy had lent itself to the late-classical and medieval concern with the relative merits of contemplative and active virtue. Macrobius associates private virtue with an otherworldly direction of mind and political virtue with the exercise of virtue in this world: "If a man is looked upon as possessing no learning but is nevertheless prudent, temperate, courageous, and just in public office, though enjoying no leisure he may

nevertheless be recognized for his exercise of the virtues of
men of action and receive his reward in the sky as well as the
others. And if a man, because of a quiet disposition, is unfit
for a life of activity but by virtue of rich gifts for introspec-
tion is elevated to the realms above and devotes the benefits
of his training solely to divine matters, searching for
heavenly truths and shunning the material world, he, too, is
taken up into the sky in consideration of his virtues of
leisure" (II.xvii.5–6). Macrobius allows the possibility of
the exemplification of these separate moral ideals by a single
person: "It often happens . . . that the same individual is
distinguished for excellence both in public life and in
private reflections, and he also is assured of a place in the
sky" (II.xvii.7). Scipio himself, like Spenser's Arthur, "belongs to that group of men who both mold their lives
according to the precepts of philosophy and support their
commonwealths with deeds of valor." Such men are
"charged with upholding the highest standards of both
modes of life" (II.xvii.9).

In epic theory private and political virtue had long been
associated with contemplation and action as the two parts of
heroic virtue. Both antinomies are implicit in the epic
formula of *sapientia et fortitudo*.[1] Fulgentius associates *arma
virumque* in the first line of the *Aeneid* with manliness
(*virtutis*) and wisdom (*sapientia*), and these in turn with the
corporeal and active on the one hand and the intellectual and
contemplative on the other (*Vergiliana continentia*, 6–10).
Tasso in the brief *Allegoria del poema* that prefaces the
Gerusalemme Liberata identifies Godfrey as Understanding
and associates with understanding contemplation; with
Rinaldo, the ireful passion, he associates the body and
action, which imply the civil life. The *Odyssey* and the
Divine Comedy, Tasso remarks, present the contemplative
man; the *Iliad* presents the man of action; the *Aeneid*,
both.

Spenser's association of political virtue with active virtue is clear from his invocation of the epic muse before the battle of Red Cross and the dragon.

> O gently come into my feeble brest,
> Come gently, but not with that mighty rage
> Wherewith the martiall troupes thou doest infest,
> And harts of great Heroës doest enrage,
> That nought their kindled courage may aswage,
> Soone as thy dreadfull trompe begins to sownd;
> The God of warre with his fiers equipage
> Thou doest awake, sleepe neuer he so sownd,
> And scared nations doest with horrour sterne astownd.
>
> Faire Goddesse lay that furious fit aside,
> Till I of warres and bloudy *Mars* do sing,
> And Briton fields with Sarazin bloud bedyde,
> Twixt that great faery Queene and Paynim king,
> That with their horrour heauen and earth did ring,
> A work of labour long, and endlesse prayse:
> But now a while let downe that haughtie string,
> And to my tunes thy second tenor rayse,
> That I this man of God his godly armes may blaze.
>
> [I.xi.6–7]

The "second tenor" of the muse is the celebration of the twelve private virtues designated for the first twelve books. Red Cross's "godly armes" are the virtues of the Christian armor mentioned by Paul in Ephesians 6 (Letter to Raleigh). Though the poet is invoking aid to depict a great combat, he carefully distinguishes its domain from that of the latter twelve books. Red Cross's career will enter the poem's domain of active virtue in the second part, when the knight of holiness fulfills his promise

> Backe to returne to that great Faerie Queene,
> And her to serue six yeares in warlike wize,
> Gainst that proud Paynim king, that workes her teene.
>
> [I.xii.18]

The first part of Spenser's plan allegorically comprises—to press the military metaphor—the arming of the knight; the second, the exercise of the arms in the arena of the world of men and nations.

The distinction of private and public virtue appears not only in Spenser's discussion of the framework of the poem he planned to write but also throughout the part of the poem that exists. It is reflected in the private and public persons of Elizabeth as embodied in Belphoebe and Gloriana (Letter to Raleigh; III.Pro.5).[2] It informs Spenser's presentation of certain of the private virtues themselves. Of Coelia it is said, "All night she spent in bidding of her bedes, / And all the day in doing good and godly deedes" (I.x.3). The enemy of the virtue of Book IV is Ate,

> mother of debate,
> And all dissention, which doth dayly grow
> Amongst fraile men, that many a publike state
> And many a priuate oft doth ouerthrow.   [IV.i.19]

The antidotes for discord in the twofold sphere of Ate's activity are Cambina's rod and cup (IV.iii.42–43), which operate in the civil and psychological realms respectively. The private-public distinction may also underlie such expressions as the "discipline / Of vertue and of ciuill vses lore" (V.Pro.3), according to which Spenser has framed his knight exemplars, and "vertuous and gentle discipline" (Letter to Raleigh), according to which Spenser has declared he is fashioning Arthur and the reader. In these instances and elsewhere a concern for public virtue seems to intrude upon the part of *The Faerie Queene* designated for the representation of the private virtues.

Whereas medieval moral treatises gave precedence to the intellectual or speculative virtues, Renaissance humanists sided with Cicero in favoring the exercise of the virtues for the public good.[3] The shift of emphasis to active virtue is evident in the growing popularity of treatises offering advice to princes and their ministers and courtiers concerning education, political administration, and social decorum.

With the emergence of the national state, writers of conduct literature, zealous for the well-being of the commonwealth, emphasized the claims of society upon private virtue. Alexander Barclay's *Mirrour of Good Maners* presses the importance of the individual's responsibility to society, shrewdly citing Plato against the contemplative life:

> We be not borne onely for our priuate profite,
> But eche man is bounde another for to succour,
> For as prudent Plato playne doth recorde and write,
> One man for another is borne, euery houre
> And time to be ready, refusing no labour
> To comfort, to counsell and succour one another,
> Both true, glad and ready as brother vnto brother.[4]

The rationale of humanistic education—preparation for public responsibility—underlies Thomas Elyot's pedagogical program in *The Governour* and is reflected in the relatively small amount of discussion devoted to the definition and analysis of the virtues apart from their application in public duties.

With the widespread circulation of the courtesy books emerged the ideal of "civil conversation." Stefano Guazzo, author of one of the most influential of these handbooks, *La Civile Conversatione,* defines his subject and title as "an honest commendable and vertuous kinde of liuing in the world." Renaissance political treatises commonly open with a definition of civil life. Justus Lipsius begins, "I define *Ciuill life,* to be that which we leade in the societie of men, one with another, to mutuall commoditie and profit, and common use of all." To essentially the same definition of civil life, Jacques Hurault, in his beginning sentence, adds the necessity of its practice: "It is manifest that the dutie of ciuill life consisteth in dealing one with another, and that therevpon both honours and empires do depend; so as princes, kings, emperours, and soueraigne lords, doe practise the ciuill life; their Dutie lieth in the exercise thereof, their welfare commeth thence, and therevpon dependeth their preseruation."[5] The practice of the civil life is, for rulers, both a social and personal imperative. Its incumbency makes the truancies of Sidney's King Basilius and Shakespeare's Duke Prospero appear all the more strikingly derelictions of duty.

The humanist insistence on exercising the virtues in the public interest might seem to entail an emphasis upon the political virtues at the expense of personal probity. Machiavelli, in fact, does advise the ruler to be prepared to disregard the claims of personal morality in order to establish a strong, well-ordered state (*The Prince*, xv, xviii). More characteristic of English treatises offering advice to rulers is a regard for the private virtues as basic to the political and as fulfilled by them in public action. The distinction between private and public virtue is not necessarily antithetical or even generic; it may represent the phases of moral development in which the private virtues are cultivated for public benefit and earthly honor. Bryskett expounds the private moral virtues "to the end to frame a gentleman fit for ciuill conuersation, and to set him in the direct way that leadeth him to his ciuill felicitie" (p. 5). Even the private virtues have their public aspects, and reflections of the two domains of virtue within the part of *The Faerie Queene* devoted to the private moral virtues are no more a violation of Spenser's proposed scheme, as Northrop Frye has charged (p. 115), than Bryskett's treatment of private virtues in *A Discourse of Civil Life*. All virtues, including the intellectual and "priuate morall," were considered incompletely possessed until exercised for the public good.

Still, the question of whether Spenser's allegiance is to the active or the contemplative ideal has been and continues to be a crux in the interpretation of *The Faerie Queene*. The poem's reflection of both ideals was accounted for by Edwin Greenlaw as an example of the Renaissance synthesis, which to understand with "all its applications to the thought of the period is to understand the Renaissance mind."[6] Robert Ellrodt seems to adjust his view to particular exigencies of his argument. When arguing against the existence of a sustained neoplatonic level of meaning in the poem, Ellrodt stresses the concern of the poem with earthly responsibility and therefore with active virtue (pp. 58–59). Later, in pointing up the medieval, rather than Renaissance (Florentine and Genevan), origins of Spenser's metaphysics, he shifts his stance and regards the renunciation of the world as more characteristic of Spenser's thought. Actually the ideals of contemplation and action are fused, Ellrodt thinks, into a "medieval duality" of perspectives, in which the claims of action are valid up to the point of the necessity, in respect to the ultimate values of eternity, of acknowledging the higher good of contemplation (pp. 208–9). Spenser's apparently contradictory position can be better understood, I think, through a clarification of terms. Greenlaw was considering Spenser's view of the relative importance of contemplation and action with respect to earthly responsibility, and Ellrodt, in the latter instance, is considering Spenser's view of these ideals with respect to the value of the rewards they bestow.

In the context of rewards, even a zealous humanist like Bryskett does not hesitate to prefer inward felicity to outward honor as the ground of virtuous action: "For vertue hath two sorts of rewards: the one that is outward, and that is honour (which cometh from others that honor vertue, and is not in the vertuous man himselfe): the other inward, which is felicitie, the true and perfectest end of all our vertuous actions whiles we are aliue" (p. 224; see also Cicero, *De officiis,* I.xxi). If earthly felicity be preferable to earthly honor, so much the more is heavenly felicity to be preferred to the honor of men. And yet, while acknowledging as much, Spenser emphasizes the worthiness of active virtue in the service of earthly honor, especially since true honor is a manifestation of the approval of heaven. Though

the New Jerusalem, as the dwelling place of the saints
"Wherein eternall peace and happinesse doth dwell"
(I.x.55), far surpasses any earthly felicity,

> Yet is *Cleopolis* for earthly frame,
> The fairest peece, that eye beholden can:
> And well beseemes all knights of noble name,
> That couet in th' immortall booke of fame
> To be eternized, that same to haunt,
> And doen their seruice to that soueraigne Dame,
> That glorie does to them for guerdon graunt:
> For she is heauenly borne, and heauen may iustly vaunt.
>
> [I.x.59]

The immortality of the book of fame and the heavenly birth
and sanction of Gloriana and her bequest associate the cities
as a twofold expression of divine will. Cleopolis has a
heavenly mandate and therefore its proper place in the career
of a saint. The honor of Cleopolis is not of course the fame
bestowed by Lucifera but the recognition "which cometh
from others that honor vertue."

It is one thing to acknowledge the superiority of heavenly
felicity to earthly honor; it is quite another to recommend
that citizens of earth occupy themselves with the anticipation of the heavenly. In the context of duty, earthly action
must take precedence over contemplative felicity. It is
entirely proper for Red Cross to pursue, for the time being,
the quest assigned him by Gloriana. "[Thou] Well worthy
doest thy seruice for her grace, / To aide a virgin desolate
foredonne." But when he has achieved his "famous victory"
(over, presumably, the enemies of Gloriana in the later
books, as well as over the dragon in Book I), it will be time
to seek the path that leads to heavenly felicity.

> Thenceforth the suit of earthly conquest shonne,
> And wash thy hands from guilt of bloudy field:
> For bloud can nought but sin, and wars but sorrowes yield.
>
> [I.x.60]

Ellrodt finds it impossible to reconcile "guilt of bloudy field" with the ideal of active virtue (p. 208). The phrase is, I think, an allusion to David's charge to his son Solomon to build the temple: "I purposed to haue buylt an house of rest for the Arke of the couenant of the Lord, & for a footestole of our God, and haue made ready for the buylding, But God said vnto me, Thou shalt not buylde an house for my Name, because thou hast bene a mã of warre, & hast shed blood" (1 Chron. 28:2–3).[7] Nevertheless, the battles of Red Cross, like the wars of King David, are against the enemies of God and have been enjoined as the necessary prelude to heavenly felicity. The path that Contemplation points out to Red Cross is to be sought by knights who have finished their earthly warfare; it is a way which "after labours long, and sad delay, / Brings them to ioyous rest and endless blis." The vacillation of Red Cross between the New Jerusalem and Cleopolis is not between duties or between felicities but between duty and felicity; and felicity, in the words of Contemplation himself, must give way to duty, contemplation to action, until duty is fulfilled and action is consummated in the completion of the earthly mission. The conflicting impulses of Red Cross toward the heavenly and the earthly do not imply a relaxation of Spenser's primary interest in active virtue. His behavior and the view it represents are no more contradictory than the similar hesitation of Paul, who acknowledged to the Philippians, "For I am greatly in doute on bothe sides, desiring to be losed and to be with Christ, which is beste of all. Neuertheless, to abide in the flesh is more nedeful for you" (Phil. 1:23–24). Red Cross follows biblical example in postponing heavenly felicity until having performed earthly duty. His and Una's interruption of their earthly felicity (I.xii.41), like Bassanio's and Portia's, illustrates the same principle.

Spenser's devotees of the reclusive life are almost always aged men, unfit for active warfare. Archimago is, of course, a fraud, whose feverish activity after his guests have fallen asleep belies his pretense to a life of contemplation. The hermit Contemplation is a

> godly aged Sire,
> With snowy lockes adowne his shoulders shed,
> As hoarie frost with spangles doth attire
> The mossy braunches of an Oke halfe ded.   [I.x.48]

His eyes "through great age had lost their kindly sight." The association of the physical debilitation of age with the ideal of contemplation defines the period of life for which this ideal is appropriate. The hermit of Book VI, it was truly rumored, "So long as age enabled him thereto," had been

> a man of mickle name,
> Renowmed much in armes and derring doe:
> But being aged now and weary to
> Of warres delight, and worlds contentious toyle,
> The name of knighthood he did disauow,
> And hanging vp his armes and warlike spoyle,
> From all this worlds incombraunce did himselfe assoyle.
> [VI.v.37]

His history parallels the career ordained for Red Cross in his successive pursuits of earthly honor and heavenly felicity.

The hermitages of Books I and VI serve as hospitals for the restoration of strength in preparation for action; they are not, for the visiting knights, permanent resting places. Red Cross, "whenas himselfe he gan to find, / To *Vna* back he cast him to retire," and having returned to her, "after litle rest, gan him desire, / Of her aduenture mindfull for to bee" (I.x.68). Having committed Timias and Serena to the care of the hermit, Arthur, "whom great affaires in mynd / Would not permit, to make there lenger stay, / Was forced there to leaue them both behynd" (VI.v.41). The etymology of *magnificence* (*magnum facere*) may not have escaped Spenser. It is "greatness of deeds" that is the work of magnificence, rather than the spiritual exercises of contemplation more appropriate to magnanimity, "greatness of soul."[8] Cer-

tainly the etymology of *Cleopolis,* "city of fame," makes clear
that the goal of the quests of the champions of virtue in *The
Faerie Queene* is earthly honor, the reward of earthly duty.
The ascent to the felicity of heavenly contemplation must
await the fulfillment of earthly responsibility, despite the
temptation for the spiritually enlightened mind to desire
with Red Cross and Paul the immediate consummation, or
at least the prolongation, of the vision of heavenly felicity.
The presence of evil in the world requires a life of virtuous
action if the enemies of virtue are not to prevail.

Of the means of inspiring virtuous action (excepting
divinity), poetry, according to Sidney, is the most effectual.
It serves directly "the highest end of the mistress Knowledge, by the Greekes called *Arkitecktonike,* which stands, (as
I think) in the knowledge of a mans selfe, in the Ethicke and
politick consideration, with the end of well dooing and not
of well knowing onely." The "ending end of all earthly
learning being vertuous action," poetry excels philosophy
and history in showing moral consequences (pp. 160–62).
The function of epic poetry in particular is to implant an
exemplar upon the mind so as to bestow, through the
emulation of that exemplar, a fleshly copy upon the world.

Only let *Aeneas* be worne in the tablet of your memory; how he
gouerneth himselfe in the ruine of his Country; in the preseruing
his old Father, and carrying away his religious ceremonies; in
obeying the Gods commandement to leaue *Dido,* though not
onely all passionate kindeness, but euen the humane consideration of vertuous gratefulnes, would haue craued other of him;
how in storms, howe in sports, howe in warre, howe in peace,
how a fugitive, how victorious, how besiedged, how besiedging,
how to strangers, howe to allyes, how to enemies, howe to his
owne; lastly, how in his inward selfe, and how in his outward
gouernment; and I thinke, in a mind not preiudiced with a
preiudicating humor, hee will be found in excellencie fruitefull.
[pp. 179–80]

The Faerie Queene accordingly offers Arthur as an example

of virtue, both "in his inward selfe" and "in his outward gouernment," which, if deeply engraved upon the mind, must produce in the reader "the ending end of all earthly learning," which is "vertuous action." Since, in the realm of earthly duty, action follows and perfects through exercise the contemplation by which the virtue was originally implanted upon the mind, the natural sequence is from contemplative, or private, to active, or public, virtue. This sequence—from "inward selfe" to "outward gouernment"—is provided for in the private-political dichotomy of the twenty-four-book scheme described in the Letter to Raleigh. It also affects the arrangement and treatment of the virtues within the sections of the poem that Spenser completed.

4 · *Complementary Association in Pairs*

The structure of *The Faerie Queene,* like that of the Elizabethan cosmos, is hierarchical. Larger units comprise systematically arranged and carefully articulated smaller units. Spenser may have intended the reader to notice the structural levels of the poem in his distribution of terminal pauses, for, as Robert Durling has observed, Books I, III (in the 1590 edition), and VI end in passages suggesting the completion of a unit of construction, and the endings of Books I, II, and VI are given greater definition and emphasis than those of the other books by the presence of exordia at the beginning of the twelfth cantos that signal the approaching conclusions of the books.[1] The effect of these authorial intrusions is to enhance the reader's awareness of the one-, two-, three-, and six-book levels of the poem's construction.[2]

This awareness has been impeded by the general tendency of recent criticism to focus upon the individual structural unit.[3] Fortunately there has been a countertendency among some critics to interpret *The Faerie Queene* in terms of the interrelations of the structural units. In particular the complementary dichotomy has been recognized as a fundamental ordering principle of Spenser's art and, as a reflection of the ancient concept of *discordia concors,* a facet of the poem's existence as an imitation of the order of the macrocosm and a pattern of the harmonious life of man, the microcosm.[4] Its importance may also be attributed to Spenser's awareness of the prevalence of binary structure in epic composition.

In the last four decades criticism of *The Faerie Queene* has increasingly tended to pair the books as complementary parts of binary units.[5] This view has obvious significance for interpretation in accounting, for example, for the deficiencies of particular virtues, or quests, in isolation. Apart from the amenability of the virtues themselves to arrangement in pairs, the allegorical links between Books I and II and between Books V and VI (in which the two quests are represented as parallel or consecutive in nature) and the narrative link between Books III and IV support their association as complementary pairs.[6]

The Letter to Raleigh offers a basis for the consideration of the books as pairs in the distinction between the natives of earth and those of Fairyland. The fairies are a separate race, ruled by Gloriana; and Arthur, born of human parentage, enters their realm in order to consummate his earthly vision. The distinction between fairy and earthling is sharpened and emphasized in the poem itself. Red Cross, as a "man of earth," is permitted to view the path to heaven, a sight denied to the fairy offspring: "Then come thou man of earth, and see the way, / That neuer yet was seene of Faeries sonne" (I.x.52). In his explanation of the relation of the New Jerusalem to earthly duty and honor, the hermit Contemplation reiterates the human origin of Red Cross.

> And thou faire ymp, sprong out from English race,
> How euer now accompted Elfins sonne,
> Well worthy doest thy seruice for her grace,
> To aide a virgin desolate foredonne.   [I.x.60]

When Red Cross has been satisfied concerning the apparently contradictory claims of heavenly felicity and earthly responsibility, he questions the Hermit further about his descent and receives a full account:

> But now aread, old father, why of late
> Didst thou behight me borne of English blood,
> Whom all a Faeries sonne doen nominate?

> That word shall I (said he) auouchen good,
> Sith to thee is vnknowne the cradle of thy brood.
>
> For well I wote, thou springst from ancient race
> Of *Saxon* kings, that haue with mightie hand
> And many bloudie battailes fought in place
> High reard their royall throne in *Britane* land,
> And vanquisht them, vnable to withstand:
> From thence a Faerie thee vnweeting reft,
> There as thou slepst in tender swadling band,
> And her base Elfin brood there for thee left.
> Such men do Chaungelings call, so chaunged by Faeries
> theft. [I.x.64–65]

The previous references to Red Cross as a fairy's son (ix.47; x.33) provide for the reader's sharing in the surprise of Red Cross, "Whom all a Faeries sonne doen nominate."

In Book II the distinction between human and fairy is strongly apparent in the divergent interests of Arthur and Guyon, a fairy by birth (II.i.6), as they become absorbed in the Briton and Elfin chronicles respectively (ix.59–60). At the beginning of Book III, the two are referred to as "the famous Briton Prince and Faerie knight" (i.1). Seven stanzas later Spenser identifies Britomart—"Whom straunge aduenture did from *Britaine* fet, / To seeke her louer"—as human. In canto iii Merlin reveals Britomart's destined role as ancestress of British kings. Her future husband, Artegall, though now in Fairyland, is also not a fairy but a human.

> He wonneth in the land of *Fayeree*,
> Yet is no *Fary* borne, ne sib at all
> To Elfes, but sprong of seed terrestriall,
> And whilome by false *Faries* stolne away,
> Whiles yet in infant cradle he did crall;
> Ne other to himselfe is knowne this day,
> But that he by an Elfe was gotten of a *Fay*. [26]

Throughout the remainder of *The Faerie Queene* an important part of the identification of the major figures is their designation as human or fairy, and Spenser employs these terms with consistency and emphasis.

The distinction appears to have structural and thematic significance. It is, one feels, no accident that the virtues of Books I, III, and V are championed by the human knights Red Cross, Britomart, and Artegall, whereas the virtues of Books II, IV, and VI are championed by the fairy knights Guyon, Cambel and Telamond (the latter, alias Priamond, Diamond, and Triamond, "all three as one," IV.ii.41), and Calidore. The repetitive unit defined by this alternating series is the pair of books, in which a virtue exemplified by a human knight is succeeded by a virtue exemplified by a fairy knight.

In *A Discourse of Civil Life* Lodowyck Bryskett speaks of the importance of properly relating the virtues to one another. He is defining true fortitude, or courage, qualifying it by the other virtues already taught the young prince. "And forasmuch as it is seldome seene, that men can use this princely vertue as it ought to be vsed, and when it should be vsed, with such other circumstances as are requisite thereto; therefore did his master instruct him and make him vnderstand, that he which matcheth not his naturall courage with Prudence, and those other vertues, which the former masters had taught him, could not rightly be called a valiant man" (p. 87). In Bryskett's discussion certain virtues define one another's bounds and are mutually dependent. They cannot be treated in isolation if the moral ideal of completeness is to be achieved. This interdependency obtains not only within the cluster of virtues around a cardinal virtue but between the cardinal virtues themselves, for Bryskett is limiting fortitude by prudence. Spenser's arrangement of the virtues in pairs seems to reflect the same conviction: that certain virtues are mutually defining and supporting and, together, form a complete conception of moral excellence in a particular area of human experience.

As Britain and Fairyland are complementary domains, of

the real and ideal, in the process of the earthly realization of the ideal, so the virtues championed by the human and fairy knights in each pair of books are mutually fulfilling in producing maturity in the particular moral relationship with which those virtues are concerned. Holiness and temperance are intrapersonal in their moral concerns and represent the domains of revealed religion and natural ethics in the quest for personal moral integrity. Chastity and friendship are interpersonal and represent the sexual and asexual kinds of attraction between persons in the quest for enduring relationships between individuals. Justice and courtesy are social and represent the domains of law and manners in the pursuit of social stability and harmony. The virtues of each pair are not antithetical but complementary in their relations, and their complementary relationship is supported by allegorical and fictional correspondences. It will be necessary to establish by detailed analysis the fact of the pairing of the books before the individual pairs may appear as part of a structural system. Having recognized the fact of the pairing and the complementarity of the virtues that are thus associated, we shall be in a position to understand the assimilative progression within each pair of books from a virtue that is a spiritual absolute to a virtue that is an ethical norm deriving from a human frame of reference and, finally, the relation of this progression to the movement of the poem from private to public virtue.

Books I and II have long been interpreted as complementary parts of a binary unit. Virgil Whitaker in 1952 observed it to be a critical commonplace and a well-established fact "that Book I and Book II show an elaborate and detailed parallelism in the sequence of episodes and that, because of their similarity, they constitute a kind of subgroup within the poem as a whole" (p. 152). The obvious correspondences may be briefly stated as follows: A knight, having been assigned a mission by the Fairy Queen, sets out with a guide. He is hindered by Archimago and Duessa, opposed by a pair of brothers (Sans Foy—Sans Joy and Pyrochles-Cymochles), weakened by prolonged confinement in the depths of the earth, rescued by Arthur, reunited with his guide, and brought to a place of instruction in the virtue he exemplifies. He then completes his quest by defeating the grand symbolic embodiment of his opposing vice.[7] The more general features of this outline have often been regarded as the intended framework of all the books, from which III, IV, and VI were to deviate.[8] It is just as plausible to regard the parallelism as having been intended to support the relation of Books I and II.

The fictional correspondences overlie a similarity of allegorical development. The careers of the titular knights are structured according to an opposition of temptations. The quest of Red Cross begins with rapid oscillations between pride and despair, which lengthen to more pronounced swings of the spiritual pendulum, culminating in the ordeals of Orgoglio's dungeon and the cave of Despair. The initial description of Red Cross suggests his potentialities for the extremes of pride and despair: the knight "of his cheere did seeme too solemne sad; / Yet nothing did he dread, but euer was ydrad" (i.2). In his encounter with Errour these potentialities are realized in the undiscerning confidence with which he enters the contest ("But full of fire and greedy hardiment, / The youthfull knight could not for ought be staide," i.14) and his failing of courage with the noxious disgorgement of the serpent ("The same so sore annoyed has the knight, / That welnigh choked with the deadly stinke, / His forces faile, ne can no longer fight," i.22). On his departure from Archimago's dwelling, we are told that "Will was his guide, and griefe led him astray" (ii.12). In his entertainment by Lucifera, Red Cross successfully resists the overt attacks of pride as worldly vanity and despair as the pagan pessimism of Sans Joy. In the dungeon of Orgoglio and the cave of Despair he very nearly succumbs to the more treacherous forms of these temptations as religious pride and religious doubt. Spenser seems to indicate that pride and despair, though apparently opposite states of mind, are closely involved with one another; for sloth, traditionally associated with despair (e.g., Chaucer's Parson's discussion of "wanhope" as a manifestation of *accidia*), is the prelude to, and despair the consequence of, the defeat by Orgoglio. The ministry of the House of Holiness is twofold, according to the nature of these related temptations. Fidelia's instruction, corrective of pride, produces a contempt for the world that would result in despair if Speranza did not complement it with hope. The discipline of the House of Penance is directed against pride, whereas the remainder of the education—supervised by Charissa and performed by Mercy, the seven Beadsmen, and Contemplation—is an antidote to despair.[9]

Guyon's first encounter with evil hints at the two kinds of temptation that will assail him in his quest. He is moved to wrath by the accusations of Archimago (i.9–13) and impressed by the pulchritude of the "Faire Ladie," whose sorrow has marred "the blossome of your beautie bright" (i.14). Guyon's opponents will represent either the irascible ("froward") or concupiscible ("forward") emotions. Guyon sees the consequences of their unrestraint in Amavia and Mordant, victims respectively of excessive grief and unbridled sensuality, and the possibility of their control in the castle of Medina. He repels the attacks of Furor and Pyrochles, on the one hand, and the overtures of Phaedria and Mammon, on the other, but falls prey to the malice of Pyrochles and Cymochles after his debilitating descent into the cave of Mammon. Rescued by Arthur, Guyon comes to Alma's castle of health, where the forward and froward passions are kept in proper balance. Thus, maturity in temperance, as in holiness, appears as an inner rectitude amidst alternating and coordinated attacks from opposite sides.

The affinity of the virtues of holiness and temperance is

emphasized by the linking episode. Archimago, having failed to destroy the knight of holiness, tries to create a breach between holiness and temperance in inciting Guyon against Red Cross. His scheme assumes the compatibility of the two virtues:

> And now exceeding griefe him ouercame,
> To see the *Redcrosse* thus aduanced hye;
> Therefore his craftie engine he did frame,
> Against his praise to stirre vp enmitye
> Of such, as vertues like mote vnto him allye.   [II.i.23]

When Guyon lowers his spear and salutes Red Cross, they are instantaneously in fellowship: "Goodly comportance each to other beare, / And entertaine themselues with court'sies meet" (i.29). On arriving at the scene, the Palmer congratulates Red Cross on his victory over the dragon and, then, associates the quests of the two knights: "But wretched we, where ye haue left your marke, / Must now anew begin, like race to runne" (i.32). Guyon's "race" parallels as well as succeeds that of Red Cross, for their virtues have a common concern—good inner government—while differing in approach and perspective.

The fellowship of the two knights and the association of their quests by the Palmer have generally been interpreted by critics as indicating the affinity not only of the two virtues but also of their ethical milieus. The dependence of Red Cross on Una, true religion, and the preponderance of biblical allusions in the Book of Holiness suggest the domain of Christian revelation. Guyon's reliance upon the Palmer, right reason, and the preponderance of references to classical writers, especially Aristotle and Virgil, in the Book of Temperance suggest the domain of natural ethics. But the meaning of Spenser's allegorical reconciliation of the two domains has been variously constructed. To H.S.V. Jones it recalls the scholastic synthesis of faith and reason. Frederick Padelford regards the linking of the two virtues as an aspect of the historical allegory: the qualification by reason of the Puritan religious zeal. "To the Puritan demand that one surrender himself exclusively to the claims of religion, Spenser opposes the Hellenic theory that all things should be done in moderation, and that life should result in an harmonious development of many powers." The most influential discussion of the relation of the domains of the two books has been A.S.P. Woodhouse's paper "Nature and Grace in *The Faerie Queene*," in which Woodhouse shows that the relation of their domains conforms to the Renaissance distinction of two moral orders, grace and nature. In this commonplace distinction of two intellectual frames of reference for the discussion of moral conduct, the orders of grace and nature were regarded as compatible, since the Author of human redemption is also the God of nature. The order of grace, however, represented the more profound revelation of God's will for man, and Woodhouse thought that eventually in *The Faerie Queene* a synthesis would have been effected in which grace was given priority over nature. Woodhouse's view was not a radical departure from previous formulations of the relation of Books I and II but rather contributed a more specific historical basis for relating their domains. His distinction lends itself to the view of the complementarity of the books as an illustration of the Christian-classical synthesis of Renaissance humanism, whose roots, as Douglas Bush has shown, penetrate deeply into the Middle Ages.[10] Spenser's linking of the books was supported by the conviction that a system of morality derived from the law of God written on the mind and exemplified in the rational morality of the ancients does not differ essentially from—and in fact provides practical support for—the morality of the inspired writers of the Scriptures.

The distinction between the ethical domains of Books I and II is anticipated in Book I in the defense of Una by the satyrs and Satyrane against Sans Loy (canto vi). Natural reason welcomes divine revelation and assumes its defense against lawlessness but without complete success. In Book II Sans Loy will appear as the extreme of the concupiscible passions that needs to be balanced by the irascible for the preservation of the virtuous mean (canto ii).[11] Lawless appetite is an enemy in degree to natural ethics, which consists of a practical compromise between competing impulses, but an enemy in kind to Christian holiness, which is absolute conformity to the will of the Supreme Lawgiver. The essence of classical temperance is rational organization of the faculties in harmonious coexistence, whereas holiness requires the denial of desires that deviate from the commandments of God.

The supernatural and natural domains of Books I and II appear vividly in a comparison of the educations of Red Cross and Guyon in their retreats for instruction in virtue. The House of Holiness provides a theological analysis of Christian righteousness, stressing the helplessness and unworthiness of the human creature on whom righteousness is bestowed as a gift of divine grace. The Castle of Alma presents an anatomy of physiological and psychological order, in which all the human faculties are performing their natural functions. The Castle is with difficulty resisting a siege carried on by the anarchic, hypertrophied impulses of the sensual nature. Arthur's role, in the rescue of Alma as well as of Guyon, is the preservation of the harmony of the natural faculties against the provocation to perverse extremes, whereas, in the rescue of Red Cross, it is the restoration of union with and conformity to divine truth. Each house, moreover, provides its visiting knight with an inspirational view of the basis of the virtue it exemplifies. Red Cross, on the Mount of Contemplation, looks into the future, whereas Guyon, in the turret, surveys the past; for Christian virtue is grounded on faith, and natural virtue on experience. Holiness furthermore has heavenly sanctions, whereas natural virtue has its sufficient justification in the accumulated examples of human history.

The common hostility of Archimago toward the knights of holiness and temperance points up the alliance of these virtues.

> For since the *Redcrosse* knight he earst did weet,
> To beene with *Guyon* knit in one consent,
> The ill, which earst to him, he now to *Guyon* ment.
>
> {II.iii.11}

His differentiation in modes of attack suggests the distinction between the domains of Books I and II. In Book I Archimago is the protean deceiver, whose shifting shapes invade the realms of all four elements: "Sometime a fowle, sometime a fish in lake, / Now like a foxe, now like a dragon fell" (I.ii.10). Here Archimago represents evil as counterfeit good in every area of human experience. In Book II the fundamental principle of evil is disorder. Guyon's opponents suggest the four elements in unrelation: Pyrochles as fire, Cymochles as water (cf. *kuma,* "wave," and the water imagery associated with sensual indulgence), Phaedria (lightness, levity, looseness) as air, and Mammon as earth.[12] Since the brothers Pyrochles and Cymochles threaten Guyon under the supervision of Archimago (canto viii), it would appear that Archimago's malice toward the knight of temperance aims at provoking a psychological anarchy analogous to the lawlessness of chaos. As Archimago's efforts in Book I are directed toward preventing that union with Truth which is holiness, in Book II Archimago strives to subvert that internal harmony or self-unity which is temperance. In Spenser's young gentleman, as in Milton's Adam, the two are clearly inseparable.

Books III and IV, like Books I and II, have long been associated in narrative technique and thematic concerns. In 1915 John Erskine noted as "a favorite explanation" of their "defects of plot" the conception "that Books III and IV are really one, that Spenser so conceived them, and that neither should be read apart from the other" (*Variorum*, 4:289). Josephine Bennett and others have regarded these books as an early stratum of the poem's composition written under the influence of Ariosto (*Evolution*, chap. 13). W.J.B. Owen regards them thus as a continuum: "In III and IV twenty-four cantos well integrated in subject-matter are arbitrarily divided into two blocks of twelve cantos each, for no good reason connected with style, tone, or narrative logic." To C. G. Osgood the books, in their thematic relations, "present themselves rather as a unit than as two separate books." More recently critics have seen in the books a unifying mythological structure: of Cupid and Psyche and of Venus and Diana. Thomas Roche follows up these suggestions in his perceptive study of the allegory of Books III and IV, in which the books appear as "a continuous twenty-four-canto unity with correspondences between each half."[13]

Though fictional correspondences are not so striking in Books III and IV as in Books I and II, there is enough symmetry to suggest that Spenser conceived the books as a pair. Whereas Book III ends with two cantos depicting the freeing of a woman sought by a man, Book IV ends with two cantos depicting the freeing of a woman seeking a man. Each has been imprisoned for seven months, within walls of fire and water respectively (Roche, p. 210). Glauce's effort to cure Britomart's love sickness (III.ii) has a counterpart in Cymodyce's attempt to remedy Marinell's disease (IV.xi). Whereas Glauce seeks out Merlin, Cymodyce consults Tryphon and Apollo.

A more obvious indication of association is the interlocking of the narratives. The love quests of Book III are fulfilled in Book IV; that is, the oppressive anxieties are relieved, though the loves are not consummated. Amoret and Scudamour are reconciled, by virtue of Scudamour's assurance of her fidelity (IV.vi). Florimell is accepted by Marinell (IV.xii). Britomart is betrothed to Artegall (IV.vi). Although there is no specific linking episode, as in the cases of Books I and II and Books V and VI, the uninterrupted flow of narrative from Book III into Book IV conveys the impression of a seamless whole.

The fictional continuity and uniformity of narrative technique should not, however, be permitted to obscure the distinction between the thematic domains of the books. In distinguishing between these domains Spenser's method is the same as in the case of Books I and II: contrast within similarity. The new thematic concern of Book IV becomes immediately apparent in the first canto with the arrangement of the characters of Book III, as well as of those introduced in Book IV, in pairs: Britomart and Amoret, Paridell and Blandamour, Duessa and Ate, and Scudamour and Glauce. In the first adventure Britomart's response to the challenge of the "iolly knight" at the castle emphasizes the concern of Book IV with human pairs: Britomart replies that "either he should neither of them haue, or both" (i. 10). She contrives that the defeated knight remain in the fellowship of the castle, "So none should be out shut, sith all of loues were fitted" (i. 12). In general, the characters that have appeared singly or in sexual pairs in Book III appear in Book IV in asexual pairings. In canto ii the arrangement of Cambell and Triamond and of Cambina and Canacee as asexual rather than sexual couples reflects the new concern of Book IV as that of friendship, or love between equals. Cambell and Triamond, who have engaged in bitter combat in the contest for Canacee, appear with their ladies as

> Two knights, that lincked rode in louely wise,
> As if they secret counsels did partake;
> And each not farre behinde him had his make,
> To weete, two Ladies of most goodly hew,
> That twixt themselues did gentle purpose make. [ii. 30]

Such sexual pairs as Britomart and Scudamour or Amoret
and Arthur are associated for nonsexual reasons—those of
friendship. It is true that the lovers Britomart and Artegall
meet, in what has been regarded as the central episode of
Book IV,[14] but they soon separate because of overriding
commitments.

> At last when all her speeches she had spent,
> And new occasion fayld her more to find,
> She left him to his fortunes gouernment,
> And backe returned with right heauie mind,
> To *Scudamour,* whom she had left behind,
> With whom she went to seeke faire *Amoret,*
> Her second care, though in another kind.   [vi.46]

Spenser's "second care," like Britomart's, is friendship; and
the claims of eros, the concern of Book III, are in the
succeeding book subordinated to the claims of philia and
agape.

Amyas's and Aemylia's misfortunes derive from their
putting the claims of erotic love before all consideration of
other ties. Aemylia censures this former disregard of friends
and family in telling her story to Amoret:

> It was my lot to loue a gentle swaine,
> Yet was he but a Squire of low degree;
> Yet was he meet, vnlesse mine eye did faine,
> By any Ladies side for Leman to haue laine.

> But for his meannesse and disparagement,
> My Sire, who me too dearely well did loue,
> Vnto my choise by no meanes would assent,
> But often did my folly fowle reproue.
> Yet nothing could my fixed mind remoue,
> But whether willed or nilled friend or foe,
> I me resolu'd the vtmost end to proue,
> And rather then my loue abandon so,
> Both sire, and friends, and all for euer to forgo. [vii.15–16]

Placidas's account to Arthur emphasizes Aemylia's resolute persistence "gainst all her friends consent" (viii.50). It is appropriate that the restoration of Amyas to Aemylia is accomplished by the agency of friendship, in the intervention of Placidas and Arthur, and forces a recognition by her of the values she had scorned. The interrelationship of "True loue and faithfull friendship" (vi.46), the domains of Books III and IV, is symbolized in the simultaneous embracing of Amyas by Aemylia, his love, and by Placidas, his friend, on his delivery from captivity:

> Whom soone as faire *Aemylia* beheld,
> And *Placidas,* they both vnto him ran,
> And him embracing fast betwixt them held,
> Striuing to comfort him all that they can,
> And kissing oft his visage pale and wan.   [ix.9]

Love and friendship are mutually supporting, if the domain of the one is not enlarged at the expense of the other.

Book IV shares with Book III the concern for permanence in relationships between individuals. All enduring ties are grounded on moral integrity, according to Spenser; for good friends must first be good men (*De amicitia*, xxvii.100), and true love is "chaste affection." The same virtuous character that gives steadfastness to Britomart's quest for Artegall and that binds their souls together in a firm covenant of betrothal requires Britomart to separate from Artegall to assist Scudamour: "For vertues onely sake, which doth beget / True loue and faithfull friendship, she by her did set" (vi.46). Beyond their common basis in virtue, however, there is a contrast in essential qualities between sexual love and friendship: sexual love properly follows Nature's norm, whereas friendship requires that which transcends Nature and is peculiarly human—an affinity of minds. Friendship is the form of love that owes nothing to physical desire and is therefore necessarily of the spirit. Being wholly of the spirit, it, to a greater extent than love between the sexes or love of kin, is immune to the depredations of time.

> For naturall affection soon doth cesse,
> And quenched is with *Cupids* greater flame:
> But faithfull friendship doth them both suppresse,
> And them with maystring discipline doth tame,
> Through thoughts aspyring to eternall fame.
> For as the soule doth rule the earthly masse,
> And all the seruice of the bodie frame,
> So loue of soule doth loue of bodie passe,
> No lesse then perfect gold surmounts the meanest brasse.
>
> [IV.ix.2]

Accordingly, the education of Amoret in the Garden of Adonis is in Nature's norm: it is "So faire a place, as Nature can deuize" (III.vi.29). It is a place where sexual union is uninhibited:

> Franckly each paramour his leman knowes,
> Each bird his mate, ne any does enuie
> Their goodly meriment, and gay felicitie.   [III.vi.41]

The governing imagery is anatomical, and the pleasure— entirely physical—is shared by all the creatures of earth. Time is a destructive force within the Garden. On the other hand, Scudamour's education, the lack of which has caused his difficulties with Amoret, is in that which must be added to all human relationships, including the sexual, in order to make them uniquely human: the marriage of true minds. As friendship is the work of that faculty that elevates man above the lower creation, the island is inhabited only by human pairs of lovers. As friendship can and must be cultivated, as well as be spontaneous, and is enriched by the acquisition of moral and intellectual qualities, as well as by natural gifts, so in the Temple of Venus art completes nature:

> For all that nature by her mother wit
> Could frame in earth, and forme of substance base,

Was there, and all that nature did omit,
Art playing second natures part, supplyed it.   [IV.x.21]

The Temple, unlike the Garden, is a place of "goodly workmanship," for the virtue it exemplifies is a rational and voluntary relationship. Whereas the Garden presents an anatomical image of physical generation, the Temple is the citadel and inner sanctuary of the mind. It images states of mental resistance—Doubt, Delay, Danger—to mental union, which are eventually overcome by mental resourcefulness, sincerity, and merit.

In Book IV antilove is not primarily perverse sexual attraction (though Lust appears as a consequence of a sexual relationship that is avowedly hostile to friendship and kinship) but an emotional state that prevents mental union. With the beginning of Book IV we learn that Amoret and Scudamour have been separated by Amoret's fear (i. 1–7), whereas in Book III Amoret's captivity has been explained as the oppression of lust. Fear and jealousy do appear in Book III as motivations of a counterfeit chastity (in Florimell's flight from Arthur and Hellenore's sequestration by Malbecco), but in Book IV they are the chief enemies of that spiritual union which is friendship. As Scudamour approaches the Temple proper, he beholds the joy of "another sort / Of louers lincked in true harts consent" (IV.x.26), whose numbers include the famous pairs of biblical and classical friends.

All these and all that euer had bene tyde,
In bands of friendship, there did liue for euer,
Whose liues although decay'd, yet loues decayed neuer.
[IV.x.27]

He envies the "endlesse happinesse" of those "That being free from feare and gealosye, / Might frankely there their loues desire possesse" (x.28). It is the dissipation of such fear as Amoret's and such jealousy as Scudamour's that is represented in Scudamour's account of his adventure in the

Temple of Venus.[15] The insufficiency of Amoret's education by Venus and deliverance from Busirane by Britomart in Book III to unite husband and wife emphasizes the complementarity of the virtues of Books III and IV—chaste physical desire and "the band of vertuous mind"—in fulfilling the marriage relationship. The removal of the remaining barriers in Book IV completes at once Spenser's treatment of marriage and his account of virtuous relationships between individuals.

Books V and VI have been the last to be associated as a pair. E.M.W. Tillyard in 1954 summed up the conclusions of Spenser criticism up to that time concerning the pairing of the books: "Books One and Two are juxtaposed and counterpointed; Books Three and Four are intertwined." The other books, however, make their contributions individually (p. 287). John Arthos, two years later, conceded the justice of this schematization: "Free from the insinuations of sustained allegory we accept the contrasts of Books I and II as contrasts, and the interwoven stories of Books III and IV as a continuing enrichment, and when we come to V and VI we are quite content they should be composed as they are" (p. 196). Since 1966, with the publication of Kathleen Williams's *Spenser's World of Glass,* Donald Cheney's *Spenser's Image of Nature,* and particularly P. C. Bayley's essay "Order, Grace, and Courtesy in Spenser's World," the connections between Books V and VI have begun to be understood also.

The narrative connections are not, for the most part, so arresting as the "counterpoint" and "intertwining" of the two previous pairs. Some parallelism has been noticed in the episodes of Sanglier (v.i) and the Discourteous Knight (vi.ii), both of whom are requited for the mistreatment of their ladies and their ruthless attack on unarmed lovers whose ladies they have preferred to their own, and the Munera-Pollente and Briana-Crudor episodes (v.ii; vi.i), instances of extortion for the sake of a personal relationship. (The latter have been regarded as contrasting the correctional methods characteristic of the knights of justice and courtesy: amputation of evil and reform.) The appearance in both books of an invincible page as companion to Arthur (in Book V not only to Arthur—viii.29—but also and principally to Artegall, "Arthur's equal") has been recognized as a parallel feature. In addition Spenser may have intended the reader to notice that in the middle cantos the virtue of the titular knight, in his absence, is analyzed into complementary characters: Talus and Britomart in Book V and Calepine and the Salvage in Book VI.[16] Furthermore both Artegall and Calidore resume their quests after a period of truancy induced by the attraction of a woman.

In addition to these rather inconspicuous connections, Books V and VI, like Books I and II, have been provided with definite linking episodes.[17] At the beginning of Book VI Artegall, returning from Irena's island "yet halfe sad," meets Calidore "in trauell on his way, / Vppon an hard aduenture sore bestad" (i.4). Artegall has succeeded in restoring Irena to her throne and has begun, with the aid of Talus, the reformation of "that ragged common-weale" (v.xii.26), when his progress is interrupted by a summons to return to Cleopolis:

> But ere he could reforme it thoroughly,
> He through occasion called was away,
> To Faerie Court, that of necessity
> His course of Iustice he was forst to stay,
> And *Talus* to reuoke from the right way,
> In which he was that Realme for to redresse. [v.xii.27]

Artegall, according to Calidore, has fully succeeded in his mission (vi.i.5), which was martial and political; but his downcast appearance and the circumstance of the interruption of his efforts to civilize Irena's kingdom convey an impression of frustration and incompleteness. Calidore speaks of his own quest as having a sequential relationship to Artegall's:

> But where ye ended haue, now I begin
> To tread an endlesse trace, withouten guyde,
> Or good direction, how to enter in,
> Or how to issue forth in waies vntryde,
> In perils strange, in labours long and wide,
> In which although good Fortune me befall,
> Yet shall it not by none be testifyde.   [vi.i.6]

Evidently Calidore's quest proper may begin only when Artegall's has been accomplished and, moreover, is necessary to bring to completion the process of civilization undertaken by the knight of justice. Calidore's quest is, by nature, more difficult—endless, "withouten guyde / Or good direction"—for his adversary is as elusive and obstinate as those forms of malice that can defy with impunity the operations of justice.

Another narrative link with thematic implications appears with the intrusion of the object of Calidore's quest, the Blatant Beast (along with his complementary constituents, Envy and Detraction), into the final scene of Book V. Artegall is returning with Talus to Fairy Court. He has had to leave the unsettled society "ere he could reforme it thoroughly" (v.xii.27), for not all the inhabitants of the "ragged common-weale" have preferred the return of Irena to the rule of the usurper, Grantorto (xii.25). In this respect Artegall's achievement contrasts with Arthur's victory in the preceding canto over the invading tyrant Geryoneo, after which

> all the people, which beheld that day,
> Gan shout aloud, that vnto heauen it rong;
> And all the damzels of that towne in ray,
> Came dauncing forth, and ioyous carrols song:
> So him they led through all their streetes along,

> Crowned with girlonds of immortall baies,
> And all the vulgar did about them throng,
> To see the man, whose euerlasting praise
> They all were bound to all posterities to raise.   [v.xi.34]

Artegall instead has encountered a mixed response, and the malice of the dissident elements is represented by the two hags that beset him in the way. Envy hurls at him, from behind, a serpent which bites him, "that long the marke was to be read" (xii.39). Detraction is joined in her vituperative attack by "A dreadfull feend of gods and men ydrad" (xii.37). Their cacophonic maledictions rise to such a pitch

> That all the woods and rockes nigh to that way,
> Began to quake and tremble with dismay;
> And all the aire rebellowed againe.   [xii.41]

Talus urges Artegall to permit him to silence them, but Artegall "for nought would swerue / From his right course" (xii.43). Artegall's clear sense of "his right course" causes him to ignore their slanderous aspersions; for the pursuit of this form of injury is beyond the limits of the domain of executive justice and belongs, rather, to the domain of Book VI.

To regard Books V and VI, like Books I and II and Books III and IV, as complementary helps to answer some of the questions that readers have raised about them. Graham Hough, in his analysis of the relations of Books I and II and Books III and IV as paired and of Books V and VI as individual, concludes that "it is perhaps the one grave fault in *The Faerie Queene* that the repressive function of Justice is so much more evident than its socially harmonizing power" (*Preface,* p. 235). If Hough had recognized that Book V is, in Christie Lerch's phrase, "designedly incomplete" in Spenser's representation of the process of civilization, he might have been more at ease with it.[18] Justice and courtesy, as Spenser represents them, are complementary rather than antithetical civilizing principles, and each principle is permitted to perfect itself within, and only within, its proper sphere. Justice is not to be condemned because it cannot do the work of courtesy, for as Thomas Starkey makes clear, "Though it be so that the law of itself be not able to bring man to his perfection, nor giue him perfit reason and virtue withal, yet forasmuch as it is a mean to bring man thereto it is not utterly to be despised. For . . . it prepareth man's mind to the receiuing of virtue by profit and pleasure, pain and punishment; . . . yea, and as man is of nature formed rude and without perfit knowledge, it is necessary to haue the institution thereof, without the which all ciuil order would decay."[19] Bryskett similarly remarks that "by taking iustice from the world, all vertue must needs decay, because she is the preseruer and defender of vertue" (p. 73). Lerch accounts for the apparently simplistic forthrightness and precision of the operation of justice in Book V by the fact that political justice, by nature, may more easily realize its perfection in the world than any other virtue, since its tangible means of redress are applied to tangible problems and against tangible opposition. Moreover, "since it happens that England in the late six-teenth century seemed to Spenser's contemporaries to have almost achieved the perfection of political 'peace,' this portion of the poem comes closer than any other part of *The Faerie Queene* to merging the 'real' and the 'ideal'" (pp. 42–43).

The fact that political justice is more easily realized than the other virtues treated by Spenser does not make it less noble. Whereas modern sympathies have come some dis-tance from the view of coercive justice as benevolence, Jacques Hurault speaks for Spenser's age in declaring it the greatest benefit a king can confer upon his subjects. "Wherefore the dutie of a good king, is not only to doe no wrong to his subiects himselfe, but also to restrain others from doing them wrong, and to strain himselfe to the vttermost of his power, to do right either in his own person, or by his substituts, to such as seeke iustice at his hand. For the greatest good that can be done to any people, is to doe them right, and to punish such as doe them wrong" (p. 188). Artegall need not be condemned for his zealous and rigorous assertion of "a will perpetual and constant, which giveth to every man his right" (Ulpian's influential definition of justice in the opening paragraph of Justinian's *Digest*, quoted by Lerch, p. 22). Artegall's "vengeance" upon evil doing, Lerch points out, is in accord with Romans 13:1–6, the *locus classicus* in the Scriptures for the obedience of the subject to the higher powers (pp. 37–38). Romans 12:19—"Vengeāce is mine: I wil repaye" (a New Testament rendering of Deut. 32:35)—is applied in the Elizabethan homily on obedience to the responsibility of human ministers of justice: "This sentence we must understand to pertain also to the magistrates, which do exercise God's room in judgment and punishing by good and godly laws here in earth." [20]

And yet the Elizabethans understood that justice, with its benevolence of purpose, is not enough for the realization of the ideal community. The work of justice requires the complementary achievement of courtesy to bring us to Cleopolis. The somewhat ambivalent attitude of the Renaissance toward civil justice as both essential and noble and yet limited in its capabilities and proper sphere of exercise is evident in Sidney's definition of its function and status in the *Apology for Poetry*: "And for the Lawyer, though Ius bee the Daughter of Iustice, and Iustice the chiefe of Vertues, yet because hee seeketh to make men good rather *Formidine poenae* then *Virtutis amore*, or, to say righter, dooth not indeuour to make men good, but that their euill hurt not others, hauing no care, so hee be a good Cittizen, how bad a man he be: Therefore as our wickednesse maketh him honorable, so is hee not in the deepest trueth to stand in rancke with these who all indeuour to take naughtines away, and plant goodnesse euen in the secretest cabinet of our soules" (pp. 163–64). Jean Bodin exclaims, "What is he that professeth himself an innocent by all lawes? how strict is innocency, to bee good according to the lawe? how much larger are the rules of dutie than of law? How many things doe piety, humanity, liberalitie, iustice, and faith, challenge at our hands, the which are not inserted in the publike tables? It is manifest, that the most detestable vices, and that most corrupt a commonweale, are neuer called into iudgment."[21]

Of the vices that flourish beyond the reach of law, the root vice of envy, in particular, requires the attention of the ruler solicitous of the welfare of his kingdom. Hurault discusses "what remedies there be to defend a man from this maladie, that a man may not be enuious, nor enuied." To defeat envy in oneself, one must be "meeld, gentle, and charitable: for he that loueth men, cannot enuie them" (p. 257). Envy and its calumnious expression, detraction, must be driven out by a virtue that reaches to the emotional source of malice and, allegorically, by a champion whose mildness and generosity of spirit leave no room for ill will—namely, by a Calidore, "In whom it seemes, that gentlenesse of spright / And manners mylde were planted naturall" (VI.i.2). To defeat envy in others, one must show modesty: "as when a man that is praised, challengeth not such honour to himselfe, but referreth it ouer to those that praise him (Hurault, p. 258). Though Calidore is, like Artegall, "full stout and tall, / And well approu'd in batteilous affray, / That did him much renowme, and far his fame display," his reputation is rendered less obnoxious to his competitors by his modest demeanor. Calidore's mollifying of Coridon, his rival for the favor of Pastorella, exemplifies the modesty that refers honors to others—in this case, to a defeated opponent—

and shows its effects. After Calidore's victory over Coridon in the wrestling match,

> Then was the oaken crowne by *Pastorell*
> Giuen to *Calidore,* as his due right;
> But he, that did in courtesie excell,
> Gaue it to *Coridon,* and said he wonne it well.

> Thus did the gentle knight himselfe abeare
> Amongst that rusticke rout in all his deeds,
> That euen they, the which his riuals were,
> Could not maligne him, but commend him needs:
> For courtesie amongst the rudest breeds
> Good will and fauour. [ix.44–45]

Calidore's behavior toward Coridon is the supreme instance in Book VI of the operation of modesty on the state of mind that breeds the Blatant Beast. The passage, moreover, defines the province of courtesy as extending beyond that of "due right," the domain of justice. To subdue the Blatant Beast among subjects or among friends, the ruler or the citizen must "in courtesie excell" the legal obligations of justice by kindness and humility. Courtesy elicits "good will and fauour" from the elements of society—"the rudest"—that justice can only antagonize and alienate by physical constraint.

Renaissance political philosophers gave a great deal of thought to the problem of public morality beyond the domain of law. Frequently their discussion led them to a consideration of the Roman use of censors to control social evils not proscribed by the laws.[22] The method of correction employed by the censor, according to Cicero, is reproof and shame: "The censor's judgment imposes almost no penalty except a blush upon the man he condemns. Therefore, as his decision affects nothing but the reputation, his condemnation is called 'ignominy.'"[23] Lipsius's discussion of the role of a censor defines the domain of public morality beyond

law, which he calls "manners," and emphasizes its importance to the state:

I tearme this office of a Censor to be A punishment concerning
manners, or those excesses which are not forbidden by Lawes. For
the proper dutie, thereof, is to correct those things which deserue
not to be punished, yet being neglected or continued, they
minister occasion of many great mischiefs. Yea being tollerated,
they do, by little and little, wholy subvert an estate. For what
auayleth it to play the men abroad, if we liue like beasts at home?
Truly if both dutie and shame, did not restraine euery particular
person, we should be nothing more assured, to haue heaped vp
riches euen to the skies.[24]

The instances of misconduct corrected by Calidore and
Arthur in Book VI are distinguishable from the evil doing of
Book V as forms of omitted duty toward a fellow man, yet so
highly aggravated as to become acts of brutality. Both
Briana's and Sir Turpine's inhospitality is carried to the
extreme of overt aggression. Mirabell in spurning her
suitors imposes cruel hardships upon them. Omission of
duty must be remedied by persuasion, and it is evident why
Calidore, like the Roman censor, would need the gift of
eloquence to perform his role effectively. The force of Calidore's eloquence in converting Briana contrasts with the
ineffectuality of Artegall's logic in changing the Giant's
mind or the mind of his followers (VI.i; V.ii). Calidore urges
Briana, "Then doe your selfe, for dread of shame, forgoe /
This euill manner" (VI.i.27). In the preceding stanza the
domains of Books V and VI are carefully distinguished.
Calidore's own weapon has been turned upon him by
Briana, "who with vncomely shame / Gan him salute, and
fowle vpbrayd with faulty blame" (i.24). Calidore replies,
defending his violent defeat of the Seneschal,

> Not vnto me the shame,
> But to the shamefull doer it afford.
> Bloud is no blemish; for it is no blame

To punish those, that doe deserue the same;
But they that breake bands of ciuilitie,
And wicked customes make, those do defame
Both noble armes and gentle curtesie.
No greater shame to man then inhumanitie.   [i.26]

The destruction of the Seneschal by the sword and the reproof of Briana define the domains and emphasize the compatibility and complementarity of the virtues of justice and courtesy. In Book VI shame, rather than punishment, is the typical reward and remedy of ill doing, and Calidore's words to Briana evoke the intonations of the Roman censor.

The distinction between Artegall's and Calidore's spheres of responsibility is given special clarification and emphasis by the Hercules motif in Books V and VI. It has been noticed that both Artegall and Arthur in Book V and Calidore in Book VI are linked by the nature of their adventures with Hercules as heroes of civilization.[25] The parallelism between Artegall's adventures in Book V and the career of Hercules has been worked out in detail, with minor divergencies, by Jean MacIntyre, T. K. Dunseath, and Jane Aptekar.[26] The medieval tradition of Hercules, deriving from the syncretic accounts of late-classical historiographers, depicted the hero as a founder of Western civilization and, despite his notable shortcomings, an example of heroic justice as a personal virtue. Artegall, like Hercules, extends civilization to the West in his establishing of order in Irena's kingdom. Like Hercules he must, in order to establish justice, subdue the monstrous descendants of the Titans, as well as other exemplars of injustice. On the level of personal justice, Artegall's career, like the medieval Hercules', exhibits a gradual conquest of the ignoble extremes of immoderate wrath (iii.36) and concupiscent susceptibility to the wiles of woman. The parallelism of Artegall's and Hercules' labors is fairly strict. His subduing Sir Sanglier—"Sir Wild Boar"—recalls Hercules' capture of the Eurymanthean Boar.[27] Artegall's combat with Radigund and its ignominious outcome conflate Hercules' experiences with Hippolyte, Omphale, and Iole. Artegall's and Arthur's conquest of the Souldan parallels Hercules' triumph over the tyrant Diomedes and his man-eating horses. The protean Malengin recalls Hercules' foe the shape-changing Achelous, and his crafty theft and underground lair suggest those of the robber Cacus, destroyed by Hercules for stealing and hiding his cattle. Geryoneo, slain by Arthur, is the son of Geryon, overcome by Hercules. Artegall's deliverance of Irena recalls Hercules' rescue of Hesione. Dunseath, summing up, mentions still another parallel: "From the opening encounter with Sanglier, the descendant of the Eurymanthean Boar, to the freeing of Irena-Hesione, Artegall's quest is true to the Hercules pattern. It is consistent with Spenser's poetic design that Artegall's final labor in *The Faerie Queene* be the confrontation of *Invidia*, Hercules' last opponent" (p. 232).

The confrontation of *Invidia* is indeed Herculean Artegall's, but the labor of overcoming envy and its social manifestations will be Herculean Calidore's. For, as Bayley observes, "Calidore is a kind of protraction of Artegall-Hercules" (p. 189). The two explicit references to Hercules' labors in Book VI (xii. 32,35) link Calidore's capture of the Blatant Beast with Hercules' destruction of the Lernian Hydra and his subduing of Cerberus, the guardian dog of hell. Jane Aptekar has shown that both the dog and the hydra were part of the iconography of envy (pp. 201—210). (Barking Envy appears also in Spenser's "To His Booke" that prefaces *The Shepheardes Calender*.) The cowardly, many-headed manifestations of social malice that escape Artegall's sword and Talus's flail in Book V have their source in the resentment of others' good and possess roots so profoundly involved with the emotional sources of human aggression that their extirpation requires, as it were, an assault on hell itself. Calidore's descent into the "hellish dens" (xi.41) of the thieves to deliver Pastorella, who "thought her self in hell, / Where with such damned fiends she should in darknesse dwell" (x.43), recalls Hercules' descent to rescue Alcestis. The parallel strengthens the association of Calidore's capture of the Blatant Beast with Hercules' binding of Cerberus, for the late episodes of Book VI interpret the significance of Calidore's rather perfunctory defeat of the Beast. The Blatant Beast is the offspring of Cerberus and Chimera, sent from hell "To be the plague and scourge of wretched men" (i.8). In the allegorical interpretation of Hercules' labors by the Renaissance, Hercules' return from hell with Cerberus was commonly taken to represent Christ's harrowing of hell (MacIntyre, p. 6; Bayley, p. 189; Aptekar, p. 213). There is, it seems, an echo of Christ's triumphant bursting the bars of death and hell in the description of Herculean Calidore's overpowering assault on the subterranean stronghold of the thieves:

> When to the Caue they came, they found it fast:
> But *Calidore* with huge resistlesse might,
> The dores assayled, and the locks vpbrast.   [xi.43]

Pastorella's emergence into the light of day is likened to the release of a prisoner of death: Calidore,

> forth her bringing to the ioyous light,
> Whereof she long had lackt the wishfull sight,
> Deuiz'd all goodly meanes, from her to driue
> The sad remembrance of her wretched plight.
> So her vneath at last he did reuiue,
> That long had lyen dead, and made againe aliue. [xi.50]

The rescue of Pastorella by Calidore enacts symbolically the restoration of the Golden Age society destroyed by the brigands. Its successful accomplishment is no less a labor than the harrowing of hell and dragging envy from its stronghold in the hearts of men. The defeat of the Blatant Beast allegorically recapitulates Calidore's assault on the brigands, for Calidore, fronting the gaping beast, faces a veritable hell-mouth,

> that seemed to containe
> A full good pecke within the vtmost brim,
> All set with yron teeth in raunges twaine,
> That terrifide his foes, and armed him,
> Appearing like the mouth of *Orcus* griesly grim. [xii.26]

The allusions to the labors of Hercules that accompany Calidore's defeat of the Blatant Beast point up the distinction between the responsibilities of Artegall and Calidore. While being suppressed by Calidore, the Blatant Beast raged "like a feend, right horrible in hew"

> Or like the hell-borne *Hydra,* which they faine
> That great *Alcides* whilome ouerthrew,
> After that he had labourd long in vaine,
> To crop his thousand heads, the which still new
> Forth budded, and in greater number grew. [xii.32]

Hercules "ouerthrew" the Hydra, according to Spenser's improvisation, after unsuccessfully attempting to defeat him by the sword. Calidore's application of the sword to the Beast simply infuriates him further:

> Sternely he turnd againe, when he him strooke
> With his sharpe steele, and ran at him amaine
> With open mouth. . . .   [xii.26]

Then wisely, Calidore,

> right well aware, his rage to ward,
> Did cast his shield atweene, and therewithall
> Putting his puissaunce forth, pursu'd so hard,
> That backeward he enforced him to fall.   [xii.30]

The sword is the proper weapon against evil in Book V. Jove's sword, Chrysaor, proven in the conquest of the rebellious Titans, is wielded by Artegall against their descendants. It is irresistible against tangible foes (v.i.10). At the beginning of Book V, the action of justice against vice is represented as a cropping of sprouts from a plant. In ancient times

> the wicked seede of vice
> Began to spring which shortly grew full great,
> And with their boughes the gentle plants did beat.
> But euermore some of the vertuous race
> Rose vp, inspired with heroicke heat,
> That cropt the branches of the sient base,
> And with strong hand their fruitfull rancknes did deface.
>
> [i. 1]

Artegall, wielding a strong sword in a "strong hand," is linked with Hercules and Bacchus as part of "the vertuous race" that subdued evil, though temporarily and merely in its excrescences, by amputation.[28] Calidore's mode of attack must be different; for his prey, the Blatant Beast, cannot, like Geryoneo, be overcome by dismemberment. In *The Republic* Plato declares emphatically that extralegal means must be relied upon to combat licentiousness in the domain of manners. He has Socrates say, with respect to evil customs not directly affecting the stability of the state, "I would not go on to try to legislate on such matters." Foolish reformers are "the most charming spectacle in the world when they enact and amend such laws as we just now described and are perpetually expecting to find a way of putting an end to frauds in business and in the other matters of which I was speaking because they can't see that they are in very truth trying to cut off a Hydra's head."[29] Social abuses—expressions of ill will not only toward civil authority but also between subjects themselves—must be wrestled with, bound, and muzzled by the patient application of other means of redress. Calidore "nathemore his heauy load releast, / But aye the more he rag'd, the more his powre increast" until the Beast was almost throttled (xii.32).

> At last when as he found his force to shrincke,
> And rage to quaile, he tooke a muzzell strong
> Of surest yron, made with many a lincke;
> Therewith he mured vp his mouth along,

And therein shut vp his blasphemous tong,
For neuer more defaming gentle Knight,
Or vnto louely Lady doing wrong:
And thereunto a great long chaine he tight,
With which he drew him forth, euen in his own despight.

Like as whylome, that strong *Tirynthian* swaine,
Brought forth with him the dreadfull dog of hell,
Against his will fast bound in yron chaine,
And roring horribly, did him compell
To see the hatefull sunne, that he might tell
To griesly *Pluto*, what on earth was donne,
And to the other damned ghosts, which dwell
For aye in darkenesse, which day light doth shonne.
So led this Knight his captyue with like conquest wonne.
                                    [xii. 34–35]

The description of Calidore's struggle and triumph emphatically distinguishes Calidore's means of redress from Artegall's, while indicating through the allusion to Hercules' descent into hell, the profounder levels at which the knight of courtesy must apply these means to overcome his prey.

It is appropriate that the major embodiment of vice in Book VI should be, like Hercules' victim Cerberus, a hellish dog. Cowardice is the dominant characteristic of the enemies of the social order in this book. The cowardly flight of Briana's Seneschal, the thieves, and the Blatant Beast and the sneak attack from behind by Sir Turpine and Defetto exemplify a form of evil that asserts itself only with the confidence of a carefully calculated advantage or in sudden forays from near-impregnable sanctuaries. To attempt to excise it by the sword of executive justice is only to drive it deeper into its lair and to provoke an at once more guarded and more inveterate expression of malice. Jean MacIntyre has suggested that Calidore's binding and leading on a chain the monstrous dog associates his quest with the work of Hercules Gallus, renowned for his persuasive eloquence.

She cites Alciati's emblem "Eloquentia fortitudine praestantior" and the description in *Cooper's Thesaurus* of Hercules "lyke on olde man . . . drawing after him a multitude of people, tyed by their eares with a little chayne wrought with ambre and golde." His captives "were so easily tyed, that laughing and with good cheere they willingly followed, and as it seemed, would not be loosed." The chain was fastened at the other end to the tongue of Hercules, "who looked towardes them with a laughing countenaunce." According to Thomas Wilson, in his preface to the *Arte of Rhetorique,* "such is the powere of eloquence and reason, that most men are forced, euen to yeeld in that which most standeth against their will. And therefore the Poets doe feine that *Hercules* being a man of great wisedom, had all men linked together by the eares in a chaine, to drawe them and leade them euen as he lusted" (p. 10). Though Spenser's description omits some of these details, the conspicuousness of Calidore's leading the Beast on a leash as a triumph of Hercules supports this identification (xii.37). Calidore, observes MacIntyre, is a master of penetrating eloquence: his "euery act and word, that he did say, / Was like enchantment, that through both the eares, / And both the eyes did steale the hart away" (ii.3).[30] "The maystring might / Of doughty *Calidore*" (xii.38) exhibited in the Book of Courtesy is the power of persuasion, rather than, like Artegall's in the Book of Justice, the power of physical coercion. Both must operate in their respective domains for Spenser's ideal of civil life to be fully realized.

In *Areopagitica* Milton addressed his own powers of eloquence to correcting a situation in which, he believed, the domain of law had encroached upon the domain of manners. His warning reminded the rulers of England of the problem with which all responsible governments continually grapple: "Impunity and remissness, for certain, are the bane of a commonwealth; but here the great art lies, to discern in what the law is to bid restraint and punishment, and in what things persuasion only is to work."[31] The latter realm is the sphere of operation of "courtesy," as Spenser conceived it—what Lord Moulton has called "the domain of Obedience to the Unenforceable."[32] Its frontiers on the domain of justice must be carefully defined and preserved, and each virtue must be permitted to fulfill itself to the extent, and only to the extent, of the limits of its proper jurisdiction. As justice is the foundation of the state, courtesy is "of all goodly manners . . . the ground, / And roote of ciuill conuersation" (VI.i.1). Whereas justice establishes and preserves by force the aristocratic class structure that Spenser's age considered a reflection of the divine order in nature, courtesy induces by persuasion the benevolent condescension of the superior to the inferior and generous homage of the inferior to the superior and the deferential relations between equals that grace the hierarchical society with the harmony of the divine order and enable it to work for the good of all.[33] At the beginning of canto ii of Book VI, the poet describes the social contribution of courtesy as a support of degree:

> What vertue is so fitting for a knight,
> Or for a Ladie, whom a knight should loue,
> As Curtesie, to beare themselues aright
> To all of each degree, as doth behoue?
> For whether they be placed high aboue,
> Or low beneath, yet ought they well to know
> Their good, that none them rightly may reproue
> Of rudenesse, for not yeelding what they owe.

Courtesy enables and impels the individual to relate himself properly to others in a hierarchical social system and thereby strengthens the coherence of society. This demeanor cannot be compelled by law; it must be induced by the art of persuasion.

The complementary relationship of justice and courtesy in Spenser's scheme of the virtues appears clearly in a comparison of two important episodes of Books V and VI:

Mercilla's court and the dance of the Graces on Mount Acidale. Mercilla's court, as Lerch remarks, is "a vision of Artegall's achievement" (p. 137), an imposed political calm wherein there prevails "ioyous peace and quietnesse alway, / Dealing iust iudgements, that mote not be broken / For any brybes, or threates of any to be wroken" (v.ix.24). It is, of course, the English realization of the ideal represented in the Temple of Isis. The five "louely daughters of high *Ioue*" that attend Mercilla—Justice, Wise Good Law, Mild Peace, Temperance, and Reverence—are said to mitigate Jove's wrath, but it is evident from Mercilla's judgment of Duessa that the influence of the five does not produce a wavering from the "due" of justice. Such moderation as occurs appears in the reluctant and compassionate infliction of the penalty. Whereas Mercilla's court reflects the achievement of justice—civil calm—the scene on Mount Acidale represents the triumph of courtesy—social harmony. The dance of the Graces, with its concentric circles, forms a pattern of order like that of the circumrotation of the celestial bodies around Ariadne's Crown (vi.x.12–13). The outer ring of "*Venus* Damzels" encloses an inner ring of the three chief Graces (like Mercilla's attendants, "daughters of sky-ruling Ioue"), who are encircling and bestowing their gifts upon "a countrey lasse"—"another Grace" by virtue of their ministrations. The Graces, according to E. K.'s gloss on the "April Eclogue" (ll. 109–17), "be three sisters, the daughters of Iupiter . . . otherwise called Charites, that is thanks. whom the Poetes feyned to be the Goddesses of al bountie and comelines, which therefore (as sayth Theodontius) they make three, to wete, that men first ought to be gracious and bountiful to other freely, then to receiue benefits at other mens hands curteously, and thirdly to requite them thankfully: which are three sundry Actions in liberalitye." The virtue of liberality—generosity, graciousness, and gratitude—Spenser thus makes the soul of courtesy. Accordingly, whereas Artegall is primarily an assessor

of merit, Calidore distinguishes himself at the outset as a
giver of gifts: of life to Crudor (i.42), of Crudor to Briana
(i.43–44), of Briana's castle to the Squire (i.47). Later his
referral of the honors of the wrestling contest to Coridon
shows his ability "to receiue benefits at other mens hands
curteously." Calidore's courteous response to the hospitality
of Meliboe's household exemplifies the expression of gratitude:

> Tho when they had their hunger slaked well,
> And the fayre mayd the table ta'ne away,
> The gentle Knight, as he that did excell
> In courtesie, and well could doe and say,
> For so great kindnesse as he found that day,
> Gan greatly thanke his host and his good wife. [ix.18]

Whereas the essence of civil justice is reciprocity of injury,
that of courtesy is the unmerited initiative and compound-
ing reflex of generosity. Whereas justice considers desert,
courtesy regards opportunity. Whereas justice is limited by
"due right," courtesy exceeds (as Calidore "did excell")
what is due in generous overtures of good will that elicit
even ampler responses of gratitude in an ever-widening
enveloping action of mutual benevolence.

As "goddesses of al bountie and comelines" the Graces
perform a twofold role: teaching the art of rendering the
proper respect to all of whatever rank or circumstance and
beautifying the person with the qualities that will elicit the
affectionate respect of others. Their functions are mutually
supporting in strengthening the social ties between men.
Spenser treats comeliness first and then bounty, for bounty
is a form of comeliness:

> These three on men all gracious gifts bestow,
> Which decke the body or adorne the mynde,
> To make them louely or well fauoured show,
> As comely carriage, entertainement kynde,
> Sweete semblaunt, friendly offices that bynde,

> And all the complements of curtesie:
> They teach vs, how to each degree and kynde
> We should our selues demeane, to low, to hie;
> To friends, to foes, which skill men call Ciuility. [x.23]

The Graces' two functions of bestowing comeliness and inspiring bountifulness are associated in a parallel passage in Cicero's influential *De officiis,* as translated by Nicholas Grimald (Grimald translates Cicero's *decorum* as "comeliness"): "For as the beautifulnesse of the bodie with proportionable making of the limmes mooveth a mãs yies: and deliteth them eũe with this, that al ẙ parts in a certein grace agree togyther: right so this cõelinesse that shineth abrode in our life, winneth their liking, ẘ whom we liue, by an order, stedfastnesse, & measurablenesse in all our wordes, and deedes. There must bee vsed therefore a certein reuerence towards menne, bothe to euery one of the best sorte, and also to the rest of meaner degrees. For it is not onely a signe of an arrogant body, but also of one altogither lawlesse, to be reckles, what euery man thinketh of him." [34] Whereas Artegall is a knight whose magnificent physical endowments compel universal admiration (IV.iv.42) and whereas he is not altogether "reckles, what euery man thinketh of him" ("Yet he past on, and seem'd of them to take no keepe," v.xii.42), Calidore's winsome appearance and courteous address to others—his comeliness and bountifulness—epitomize the ideal represented by the Graces.

As a support to society, courtesy is especially important in complementing justice in the personal demeanor of the prince. Rosamund Tuve remarks that the *Moralium dogma philosophorum,* a well-known medieval treatise on the virtues, "used the *De Officiis* to outline a basic division between *Severitas* and *Liberalitas*" that influenced later discussions of justice (*Allegorical Imagery,* p. 67; *De officiis,* I.vii.20). In Renaissance political treatises the *majesty* characteristic of justice must be balanced by a discreet show of familiarity if the obedience of the subjects is to be grounded in affection as well as in fear. Thomas Elyot in his translation of *Isocrates to Nicocles* advises that a prince "endeuour . . . to be bothe courtaise and of a reuerende grauitee." [35] Hurault regards "courtesie" as complementary with *majesty* in the ideal rule: "when maiestie is mingled with courtesie, there is no harmonie so perfect & musick-like as that. For it is the thing wherin the prince may resemble God, who enforceth not vs to any thing, but doth sweeten the constraint of obedience with demonstration and persuasiõ of reason" (p. 90). The word *courtesy* in Renaissance writings on justice commonly denoted Cicero's *liberalitas,* which in E. K.'s gloss designates the work of the Graces.

In Mercilla's court, Awe "with gyantlike resemblance" intimidates "guyle, and malice and despight, / That vnder shew oftimes of fayned semblance, / Are wont in Princes courts to worke great scath and hindrance" (v.ix.22). She conducts her state "in souerayne Maiestie" (ix.30). In Book VI the Graces bestow their gifts on the body and mind

> To make them louely or well fauoured show,
> As comely carriage, entertainement kynde,
> Sweete semblaunt, friendly offices that bynde. [x.23]

The contrast in atmospheres is between Awe, or majesty, that intimidates and the comeliness and bountifulness that elicit affectionate admiration and loyalty ("the friendly offices [cf. the title of Cicero's treatise] that bynde"): namely liberality, the soul of Spenserian courtesy. The receiver of the gifts of the Graces appears "as a precious gemme, / Amidst a ring most richly well enchaced, / That with her goodly presence all the rest much graced" (x.12). The effect of majesty is subjection; the work of the Graces is apotheosis, for "a countrey lasse" has become, by their gifts, "another Grace." Moreover, her presence "all the rest much graced." The circular action of the virtue of Book VI is evident in that the bounty of the Graces has begotten comeliness and bounty in the object of their ministrations, which in turn beget a bountiful response of affection and, therefore, a comeliness of demeanor in the beholders as well. This circle of benevolence is especially effectual when initiated by the conduct of the ruler. It may also be set in motion by "a countrey lasse" and spiral upward from humble levels to engage the participation of a Calidore. It is, in any case, the remedy offered by Spenser for the evils that plague society beyond the reach of justice and prevent the realization of Cleopolis.

"Manners makyth man," said William of Wyckham, and sixteenth-century Englishmen agreed. They had, moreover, a name for the moral virtue, informed by liberality, that pertains to the domain of manners. Thomas Elyot defines it as follows: "The nature and condition of man, wherin he is lasse than god almightie, and excellinge nat withstanding all other creatures in erthe, is called humanitie; which is a generall name to those vertues in whome semeth to be a mutuall concorde and loue in the nature of man. And all thoughe there be many of the said vertues, yet be there thre principall by whome humanitie is chiefly compact; benevolence, beneficence, and liberalitie, which maketh vp the said principall vertue called benignitie or gentilnes."[36] We have already identified the virtue of Book VI with *humanitas* in the comparison of Spenser's scheme of the virtues with the system of Macrobius (chap. 2). Elyot's analysis of *humanity* confirms it to be the virtue expounded in the Book of Courtesy (though differing in treating liberality as a constituent rather than a subsuming virtue). It comprises the attitudes and actions of generosity, graciousness, and gratitude that cannot be compelled by law but that are essential to the health and harmony of society. Moreover, it is by nature, as by name, the virtue that distinguishes man, in his social relations, from the lower creation. Justice, like Artegall, can impose order upon beasts, but only the mutual respect born of affectionate good will can raise men above beasts in their social relations and render their communities unique among those of the creatures of earth. The Blatant Beast is an appropriate embodiment of "inhumanitie" (VI.i.26), the antithesis of courtesy in Book VI, for it signifies the socially oppressive forms of human bestiality that prevent the advance of civilization into the domain of manners.[37]

Virgil Heltzel has suggested the virtue of *comitas* as perhaps the original of Spenser's courtesy on the basis of a passage in Haly Heron's *A Newe Discourse of Morall Philosophie*. Concerning *comitas*, Heron writes, "So agreeable to the nature of mankinde is thys gentle affection, that by the consente of sage men, it hathe bin called Humanitie, and since by the friendlye corruption of the common sorte (as I gesse) from the Courte, it nowe taketh the name of courtesie: but wee wyll not stande so much vppon the name, as the perfecte vse heereof, although in deede of late, amongst oure Englishe Poets hathe risen a doubtefull controuersie, as touching the true christening of thys Vertue."[38] A more natural inference concerning the identity of the virtue of Book VI is the association of the learned "Humanitie" and the popular "courtesie." The *humanity* of Renaissance moral philosophy evidently was popularly designated "courtesy." Of the two names for this virtue, courtesy, with its richness of connotation and its informing principle of liberality, was the right one for Spenser's purposes.[39]

Clearly the juxtaposing of justice and courtesy by Spenser was a triple expedient. First, the nature and function of justice cannot be formulated without reference to its common boundary with manners. Second, the harsh role of justice is likely not to be emotionally accepted without a recognition that it must and will be limited and complemented by the operation of persuasion in the realm of manners. Third, Spenser was representing in the allegory of the two books an ideal of civil life that he wished to be realized in the commonwealth of England. An index of the moral greatness of a society, according to an eminent modern jurist, is the extent to which the borderland of law may be safely entrusted to the rule of persuasion (J. F. Moulton, p. 1). Underlying the didactic program of Books V and VI is the recognition of the precarious existence of the domain of manners in sixteenth-century England and a desire to establish its domain in relation to that of law. The impediment to this purpose is, of course, the Blatant Beast. For as long as the domain of manners is the sanctuary of the Blatant Beast, with all the obnoxious social cacophony that it represents, justice must compensate by extending its frontiers to their furthest defensible limits and jealously guarding against any encroachment. In such a case, the nation can hardly be said to be civilized. In Spenser's England justice had completed its major work, and it remained for its complementary civilizing principle of courtesy to dislodge by comeliness and bountifulness the residual covert rebelliousness, as well as the resentment that necessarily attends the coercive action of justice, from the hearts of the refractory elements of Elizabeth's kingdom.

5 · *Cumulative Progression within Pairs*

Not only do Britain and Fairyland have a complementary relationship as the realms of the real and the ideal, but they also have a cumulative relationship as the domains of nature and nurture. The quest of the human knight takes him from the land of his birth to Fairyland, the realm of his education, where his native gifts are asserted in such a way as to be tested and disciplined to perfection. The pairing of the books according to the human-fairy dichotomy thus provides for cumulative as well as complementary relations within each pair. It should not therefore be surprising that concurrent with the process of associating and distinguishing between the milieus of the paired virtues there appears a single, sustained movement throughout each pair of books representing progress by phases toward a particular kind of moral excellence.

In the pairings of Books I and II and Books III and IV critics have seen a single movement in which the second virtue is assimilated to the first in a progression toward a more comprehensive and sufficient conception. Harry Berger and Maurice Evans have interpreted Book II as a criticism of the classical ideal of temperance, in which, as Evans remarks, Guyon "from the start . . . is placed in situations which suggest with some irony the human weakness of which he is still ignorant."[1] According to Berger and Evans, Guyon's career demonstrates the ineffectuality of the ethical doctrine of the mean and the necessity of denying, rather than merely moderating, vicious impulses with the assistance of divine grace. Guyon's helplessness in Mammon's delve and the providential intervention of the angel and Arthur represent, by this view, Spenser's repudiation of the classical ideal of temperance in favor of Christian continence.

But in the Castle of Alma, the allegorical core of Book II, Arthur himself, along with Guyon, will learn the art of moderating the irascible and concupiscible passions; and enroute to the Bower of Bliss, Guyon, through the Palmer's helmsmanship, will shun vicious opposites by holding a middle course (xii. 3–29). Moreover, as Rosamund Tuve has pointed out, temperance and continence were not opposed in medieval thought, for continence was a branch of temperance (*Allegorical Imagery,* p. 131). Temperance was regarded as a Christian virtue in the Middle Ages, just as continence was a classical virtue discussed by Aristotle in the *Ethics*. Much of the modern difficulty in reconciling the idea of the mean, as moderation, with continence, as abstention, may be removed by Bryskett's explanation of Aristotle's doctrine of the mean: "And therefore Aristotle said right well that the meane of vertue betweene two extremes was a *Geometricall* meane which hath a respect to proportion, and not an *Arithmeticall* meane which respecteth equall distance; so as you must understand that vertue is not called a meane betweene two extremes, because she participateth of either of them both, but because she is neither the one nor the other" (p. 210). In Book II unrestraint of the concupiscible and irascible passions perverts them from their natural order and function; and it is these unnatural extremes, exemplified in Pyrochles and Cymochles, rather than the properly harmonized forms, appearing in the "louely beuy of faire Ladies" in Alma's Castle (ix. 34–36), that are the vicious opposites that must be shunned by proper control. With moderation the opposites are no longer vicious, being no longer perverse, but essential to life and health; and they represent not modes of behavior but points of reference for charting the mean.

It is more accurate to see the Christian coloring of temperance as present from the beginning of Book II. Guyon recognizes in the symbol on the shield of Red Cross "The sacred badge of my Redeemers death" (i.27). On approaching Red Cross, the Palmer "Eft soones of him had perfect cognizance" (i.31) and blessed him and "that deare Crosse vpon your shield deuizd, / Wherewith aboue all knights ye goodly seeme aguizd" (i.31). This recognition of the identity of Red Cross and of the significance of the cross emblazoned on his shield surely signifies the affinity of the two virtues of Books I and II; but the homage offered by Guyon and the Palmer to the sacred insignia indicates also their awareness of an indebtedness to holiness that makes their quest dependent upon the quest of Book I. Though Guyon's steps are directed by his guide "with reason," the Palmer, by name, must be identified as Cicero's right reason returned from Jerusalem (Nelson, p. 179). The Palmer at first appears helpless to prevent the sons of Acrates from despoiling the fallen Guyon of his armor, but his rhetoric does ward off their attack until the arrival of Arthur. Also, the Palmer assists the beleaguered Arthur by providing him with Guyon's sword. Thus he is if not causal at least instrumental in the defeat of the vicious extremes represented by Pyrochles and Cymochles. In this incident, as throughout the remainder of Guyon's quest, the Palmer discharges the responsibility laid on him by the angel "Of his deare safetie" (viii.8), though, says the angel,

> Yet will I not forgoe, ne yet forget
> The care thereof my selfe vnto the end,
> But euermore him succour, and defend
> Against his foe and mine.   [viii.8]

The helplessness of Guyon and the apparent helplessness of the Palmer in Mammon's delve do not indicate the ineffectuality of temperance as a virtue of moderation but rather show the presumptuousness of the ethical ideal of self-sufficiency and the dependence of temperance upon the resources of Book I.

As a sequel to the quest of Red Cross, Guyon's quest extends the achievements of Red Cross into the domain of practical conduct. It carries forward the central themes of Book I and assimilates them with the concern of temperance. The final incident of Book II, the destruction of the Bower of Bliss, climaxes the thematic development not only of Book II but of both books of the pair. A. B. Giamatti has observed that both Red Cross's and Guyon's quests are directed toward a garden: Eden and "Bliss," a true and a false paradise (p. 249). Phaedria's island (II.vi) and the Garden of Proserpina (II.vii) parody Eden as anticipations of the arch-counterfeit, the Bower of Bliss, "inhabited by a depraved Eve, where all mankind can be induced 'to fall' " (p. 271). The invitation to ease in the rhetoric of Despair (I.ix) anticipates the temptations of Phaedria and the Idle Lake (II.vi), the silver stool in the Garden of Proserpina (II.vii), the song of the mermaids in the Port of Rest (xii.31–33), and the carpe diem song in the Bower of Bliss (II.xii.74–75). The enchanted cup of Duessa (I.viii.14), antithesis of Fidelia's cup (I.x.13), has its counterpart in the cup of Excesse (II.xii.56–57). The image of the prostrate, unarmed warrior, overcome by the charms of a witch, that epitomizes the spiritual debilitation of Red Cross (I.vii.2–7) reappears in the careless slumber of Cymochles (II.vi.14) and even more vividly in the figure of the sleeping Verdant in the Bower of Bliss (II.xii.79–80). The false Genius, Pleasure's Porter, is, like Archimago, an enchanter "That secretly doth vs procure to fall, / Through guilefull semblaunts, which he makes vs see" (II.xii.48). His collaboration with the witch Acrasia recalls that of Archimago and Duessa in Book I. The Bower of Bliss is, as Hamilton argues, a comprehensive image of all the pictures of seductive illusion that appear in Books I and II.[2] The physical temptations that in Book I are symbolic of religious infidelity are defeated in Book II as emotional impulses that through unrestraint have become enemies of the soul; and this defeat is carried out by the force of temperance, supported by redeemed reason. The biblical admonition to add to one's faith (among other things) temperance (2 Pet. 1:5–7) may have reinforced the Renaissance Christian humanist in his conviction of the efficacy of the interaction of the virtues of Books I and II and of the possibility of cumulative synthesis.

In Books III and IV the cumulative progression is more obvious; for the emerging conception of friendship as *concordia* includes both *eros* and *philia,* as well as other types of human love.[3] Both fraternal and sexual love motivate Cambina in her peacemaking between her brother, Triamond, and her lover, Cambell (IV.iii.46), just as both fraternal and sexual love had motivated the brothers Priamond, Diamond, and Triamond in their fight against Cambell. Her action harmonizes into a single bond of friendship the now mutually supporting, whereas formerly mutually opposing, forces of fraternal and sexual love. "True friendship," declares Bryskett, "tieth (though with diuers respects) children to their parents, kinred to kinred, the husband to the wife, and the minds of men of valour & virtue fast together, as a thing agreeable to all the qualities which our soule containeth" (p. 226). Friendship, however, is not simply a composite of all kinds of attraction between human beings but rather the special affinity that gives permanence to all human ties: "a communion and knitting together of minds, which neither length of time, distance of place, great prosperitie, nor great aduersitie, ne yet any other grieuous accident may seuer or separate" (p. 224). As spiritual union, friendship is a manifestation of the binding principle of the universe, whose opposite is discord of whatever form. Cicero recalls that Empedocles reportedly said, "In nature and the entire universe whatever things are at rest and whatever are in motion are united by friendship and scattered by discord." He adds, "And indeed this is a statement which all men not only understand but also approve."[4] The ancient concept of friendship as a cosmic force is probably alluded to in the title of Book IV, "The Legend of Cambel and Telamond, or Of Friendship." *Telamond,* Roche suggests, means "perfect world" (pp. 16–17) and therefore indicates the larger conception of the virtue of Book IV as a principle of universal cohesion and harmony uniting three worlds: macrocosmically, the terrestrial, celestial, and supercelestial; microcosmically, the vegetable, sensitive, and rational. Telamond is Triamond after the union of his soul with the souls of the other sons of Agape. This union of souls is a microcosmic instance of the function of friendship in the universe.

The girdle of Florimell, an emblem of the restraint of lust in Book III (e.g., vii.30–36), is associated in Book IV with the cessation of hostilities and is conferred as both a test and a reward of virtue (v.2–6). It has become in Book IV "the band of vertuous mind" (ix.1), an emblem of the moral quality that makes possible the firmness and endurance of all human relationships. As friendship, the union of souls, is essential to the permanence of all human love, so moral integrity is essential to friendship: Virtue "both creates the bond of friendship and preserves it. For in Virtue is complete harmony, in her is permanence, in her is fidelity; and when she has raised her head and shown her own light and has seen and recognized the same light in another, she moves toward it and in turn receives its beams" (*De amicitia,* xxvii.100). The sequence of winners of the three-day tournament for Florimell's girdle reinforces the cumulative synthesis of the two books on the basis of "the band of vertuous mind." After Satyrane (natural chastity) and Triamond (natural friendship as kinship) have won on the previous days, Britomart prevails on the third day and is offered the prize: the girdle and the woman who can wear it. The worthiness of Britomart, champion of Book III, to be awarded a symbol of that which is basic to the virtue of Book IV (ii.29; ix.1) associates the virtues of both books in terms of a common basis: "the vertuous mind." Her superseding of Satyrane and Triamond as chief in the tournament indicates her exemplification of an emerging conception that subsumes both the particular concerns of Books III and IV: permanency in human love. This permanency depends upon the moral rectitude of equal minds. In Book III in the unstable union of Hellenore and Malbecco, "Vnfitly yokt together in one teeme" (ix.6), and that of Hellenore and Paridell, "a wanton paire / Of louers loosely knit" (x.16), the poem presents sexual pairs related on bases other than that of the virtuous mind; and their instability contrasts with the tenacity with which Britomart, like Amoret and Florimell, seeks her lover.

Florimell's girdle is described in Book IV as conferring "the virtue of chast loue, / And wiuehood true, to all that did it beare" but also as disclosing the opposite:

> But whosoeuer contrarie doth proue,
> Might not the same about her middle weare,
> But it would loose, or else a sunder teare.
> Whilome it was (as Faeries wont report)
> Dame *Venus* girdle, by her steemed deare,
> What time she vsd to liue in wiuely sort;
> But layd aside, when so she vsd her looser sport.   [v.3]

The contrast presented is between fidelity and infidelity in marriage. The extension of the love quests of Book III into Book IV provides for representing the sequential contributions of the virtues of the books to maturity in love in terms of courtship and marriage.[5] Marriage must be a friendship if it is to flourish and endure.[6] Accordingly, Britomart's quest, directed toward marriage, is not fulfilled in Book III but passes into Book IV, where it takes the form of the acquisition and demonstration of the qualities of friendship necessary to the perfection of sexual love in marriage. In

Book IV the consent of Britomart and Artegall to marry is spoken of as "that accord" (vi.41). Having secured the assurance of Artegall's love and of his intention to marry her, Britomart takes on herself the business of friendship. Friendship, like Amoret, is "Her second care, though in another kind" (IV.vi.46). This "second care," like the first, she assumes "For vertues onely sake, which doth beget / True loue and faithfull friendship" (IV.vi.46). In Book IV, through the assistance of Britomart, Amoret is able to conquer her fear to the extent of traveling with Arthur (ix.17–19), and Scudamour overcomes his jealousy on receiving assurance of Amoret's fidelity. Amoret's anxiety in the company of Britomart at the beginning of Book IV is a transfer of her fears concerning Busirane to a situation in which they are quite inappropriate. Amoret realizes her debt to the young warrior but fears "his will." When Britomart reveals herself to be of the same sex as—an equal with—Amoret, the poem describes Amoret's response in such a way as to indicate the function of friendship in clearing away the obstacles to the fulfillment of love in marriage.

> And eke fayre *Amoret* now freed from feare,
>   More franke affection did to her afford,
>   And to her bed, which she was wont forbeare,
> Now freely drew, and found right safe assurance theare.
>
> [i.15]

The response of Amoret to Britomart's offer of companionship signifies the resolution of her fears concerning Busirane in the context of marriage by the confidence inspired by friendship.

The obstacle of Scudamour's jealousy still remains to prevent the fulfillment of Amoret and Scudamour's love. Britomart again is the agent of reconciliation, and her final resolution of the difficulties of Amoret and Scudamour coincides with the fulfillment of her own quest for Artegall

(IV.vi). Scudamour and Artegall, companions in arms against Britomart for her having stolen their lady (Amoret, wife of Scudamour and prize of the tournament), exemplify the jealousy that, as a species of immaturity in love, prevents the union of minds in marriage. The revelation of Britomart's identity in her fight with Artegall is, for Scudamour, a revelation of the innocuous nature of Britomart's relationship with Amoret. The recognition of their friendship reconciles his estranged mind to Amoret's:

> So all that euer yet I haue endured,
> I count as naught, and tread downe vnder feet,
> Since of my loue at length I rest assured,
> That to disloyalty she will not be allured.   [x.2]

The resolution of both Amoret's fear and Scudamour's jealousy is produced by revelations of Britomart's identity, which disclose her intentions of friendship. Britomart's determination, after her fight with and betrothal to Artegall, to accompany Scudamour in his search for Amoret (vi.46) is an instance of friendship's assistance of married love that complements that of her earlier travels with Amoret. Thus not only is Britomart's quest in Book IV the acquisition for her of the qualities that will cause her own marriage to prosper, but Britomart herself becomes an agent of these qualities in the quests of others whose marriage relationship is suffering from the lack of them. Finally, Britomart's function as an agent of concord in Book IV is pointed up in her subduing of Artegall, the epitome of martial prowess, by love; for it evoked for the educated Renaissance reader the conquest of Mars by Venus, emblematic of concord (Wind, pp. 81–88).

With a single stroke of Artegall's sword Scudamour is reunited, in mind, with Amoret, and Artegall is united with Britomart; and two of the principal love quests of Book III are fulfilled in respect to the concern of Books III and IV: the establishment of enduring love relationships between individuals. Likewise the quests of Florimell and Marinell continue into Book IV and find their fulfillment in mutual assurance and consent to marry. Florimell's fears and Marinell's pride (or his mother's fear) are eventually resolved by Florimell's fidelity and the circumstance of the wedding feast for the marriage of the Thames and the Medway in the house of Proteus. The circumstance, the marriage of the rivers, not only provides the resolution of a strand of plot connecting Books III and IV but also reinforces the sequential relations of the books, in respect to the love quests, as representing the phases of courtship and marriage.

> Long had the *Thames* (as we in records reed)
> Before that day her wooed to his bed;
> But the proud Nymph would for no worldly meed,
> Nor no entreatie to his loue be led;
> Till now at last relenting, she to him was wed.   [xi.8]

Book IV, in the quests of the three sets of lovers, is concerned with the resolution of mental obstacles—pride, fear, jealousy—to the fulfillment of love in marriage; and the movement from immaturity to maturity in love, from courtship to marriage, that spans Books III and IV appropriately culminates in the celebration of a marriage that produces a union not only of lovers but of families, neighbors, and well-wishing friends. The hierarchical principle implicit in the system of rivers and their tributaries reflects the divine order not only in society but also in the natural creation: "Yet were they all in order, as befell, / According their degrees disposed well" (xii.3). Concluding Book IV is an emblem of concord that unites Books III and IV as phases of a single, cumulative progression toward not only the fulfillment of sexual love in marriage but also a view of the binding force in human relationships as a manifestation of the principle that holds the universe in harmonious order.

These relations of Books III and IV are especially evident

in a comparison of the allegorical cores of the books, the Garden of Adonis and the Temple of Venus.[7] Both paradises are sacred to Venus: in the one she is the patroness of fruitful physical union; in the other, primarily of spiritual union, though her previous function is recalled by the presence on the island of pairs of sexual lovers as well as friends and by the hymn to Venus sung by one of her petitioners. Both sexual lovers and friends are united by the marriage of true minds. Whereas the foe of love and life in the Garden of Adonis is physical lust, symbolized by the chained boar, in the Temple of Venus it is those discordant states of mind that have troubled Amoret and Scudamour, Florimell and Marinell, and even Britomart and Artegall, as well as the Medway, and which have been transcended by those pairs of lovers whose bliss Scudamour wishes for himself:

> I thought there was none other heauen then this;
> And gan their endlesse happinesse enuye,
> That being free from feare and gealosye,
> Might frankely there their loues desire possesse. [x.28]

Whereas Genius, god of generation, is the porter of the gate to the Garden of Adonis, Lady Concord guards the entrance to the Temple of Venus, for spiritual harmony is the prerequisite to the pleasures represented in the paradise of Book IV. As in the Garden of Adonis the reader has been educated through the experience of Amoret in Nature's norm, in the Temple he is educated through Scudamour's experience in what must be added to the work of Nature for human love to be perfected.

Whereas the general formal features of the Garden of Adonis are those of the female reproductive system, the Temple of Venus, in relation to the love quests, represents the virgin mind. Whereas the former justifies human sexuality in terms of universal generation, the Temple of Venus shows the marriage of minds, both of sexual lovers and friends, in relation to universal harmony. The Temple of

Venus is, in particular, the citadel of the woman's mind to be won by gentle but persistent male siege. Its opposite is the House of Busirane, whose three doors and three rooms correspond to the three gates and stages of access in the approach to the island containing the temple.[8] The approach to the Temple of Venus is hindered by tempestuous passions, which must be quelled by a combination of boldness and restraint. The passions are not wholly those of the Mask of Cupid; the dissimilarity is most observable in the latter part of Cupid's procession (III.xii.24–25), which signifies the consequences of false love in famous examples of the past. Britomart forces her way into a troubled female mind, whose view of marriage has been distorted by examples of pagan love; she is bold but not too bold. Scudamour, proleptically having learned from her example in Book III, wins entrance into the Temple of Venus by his earnestness and sincerity (his shield proclaims him "Cupid's man"). He makes his way past the normal psychological obstacles to the marriage of minds and enters into the sanctuary of a virgin mind in repose, a mind cultivated in the virtues of mature wifehood: Shamefastnesse, Cherefulnesse, Modestie, Curtesie, Silence, and Obedience (x.49–52). Scudamour's success signifies the conquest of the mind that not only initiates friendship but also is the chief goal of man's courtship of woman. As the island is the handiwork of art as well as of nature, so marriage is an institution shaped not only by natural impulses but also by tradition: it is a temple "faire and auncient" (x.5). The union represented by the temple involves, as a concomitant, the fruitful physical pleasures of the Garden of Adonis but derives its essentially human quality and its enduring strength from the conjunction of minds. In pursuing his goal, the mature lover is paying court not only to the virgin mind of his beloved but also to the principle of universal concord, represented by the hermaphrodite Venus, that both unites and, in joining sexual opposites, conserves the creation. The episode justifies love between man and woman as well as love between friends as aspects of the cohesive principle of the universe and therefore of the divine will for creation.

The cumulative thematic progression of Books V and VI has been implicit in much of the evidence offered for their complementarity in chapter 4. The sequential relation of Artegall's and Calidore's quests (VI.i.6) implies the dependency of the achievement of courtesy upon the prior achievement of justice. The culmination of the subterranean imagery of Books V and VI—the cave motif as exemplified in the underground dwellings of Malengin and Geryoneo's monster—in the hell-like recesses of the brigands' lair completes a pattern of the pursuit of ever more stubbornly entrenched forms of evil at increasingly profound levels of human action and gives special point to the comparison of Calidore's defeat of the Blatant Beast with Hercules' capture of Cerberus, watchdog of hell.[9] The thieves have a comprehensive significance as enemies of both justice and courtesy, and their behavior is the antithesis of the ideal of civil life developed cumulatively throughout Books V and VI. Another motif, the chasing of savage beasts, supports the cumulative relations of Books V and VI. The young Artegall's practice of justice upon the beasts of the forest (V.i.7) prepared him for his later quest against the bestial tyrants that suppress justice in Book V. In Book VI the chasing of beasts is even more explicitly involved with the conquest of evil. Calidore's eventual defeat of the Blatant Beast has been anticipated by his subduing of the tiger (x.34–36) and Calepine's conquest of the bear (iv.17–22). Ironically counterpointing Calepine's victory in the same canto is the Salvage Man's chasing of Sir Turpine, in which a gentle savage pursues a bestial gentleman. The chasing-of-beasts motif, though appearing earlier in *The Faerie Queene,* surfaces strongly in the last pair of books as a structural element and culminates in Calidore's defeat of the Blatant Beast at the end of Book VI. The effect of the description of Calidore's overtaking of the beast is that of a highly elusive form of evil—residual despite the efforts of the champions to destroy it—finally cornered and forced to stand defeat. The chase motif presents militant virtue arrayed against that in man which precludes the possibility of civilization—indeed, of any social community worthy of the name—and which prevents his social relations from rising above the level of the animal communities. Calidore's quest continues Artegall's attack at deeper levels against those impulses of man's bestial nature that inhibit the achievements of his rational soul.

In their cumulative relationship, Books V and VI show a single, sustained movement of qualifying justice absolute. Modern readers tend to find Book V unsatisfactory because of their failure to understand the character of Spenserian justice as necessary, benevolent, and honorable, but requiring complementation. Spenser follows medieval moral philosophy in including in a comprehensive view of justice *clementia, misericordia,* and *liberalitas* (Tuve, *Allegorical Imagery,* p. 67) and legal philosophy in complementing the strict justice of law with equity. Book V begins with a simple conception of justice, embodied in Artegall as justice and Talus as the executive force of the law.[10] Their administration of justice in the early cantos is marked by strictness of procedure, exactitude in assessing merit, and severity in execution of punishment. The problems confronted by Artegall are relatively clear cut, and the narrative does not condemn the rigor of his response to these instances of injustice. In fact Artegall's defeat by Radigund is due to insufficient, rather than excessive, rigor in prosecuting his role of repressive justice. Artegall dissociates himself from Talus in accepting the challenge of single combat and, perforce, during his confinement as a prisoner of Radigund, rather than permitting Talus to fulfill his proper function. During Artegall's absence from the narrative (cantos v and vi), the poem enlarges the conception of justice to include equity by substituting for Artegall as ministers of justice the complementary figures of Talus (law) and Britomart (equity).

The Temple of Isis episode clarifies the allegorical significance of Britomart's relationship to Artegall in Book V by identifying her with Isis, wife of Osiris, god of Justice.

> His wife was *Isis,* whom they likewise made
> A Goddesse of great powre and soverainty,
> And in her person cunningly did shade
> That part of Iustice, which is Equity,
> Whereof I haue to treat here presently.
> Vnto whose temple when as *Britomart*
> Arriued, shee with great humility
> Did enter in, ne would that night depart;
> But *Talus* mote not be admitted to her part.
>
> There she receiued was in goodly wize
> Of many Priests, which duely did attend
> Vppon the rites and daily sacrifize,
> All clad in linnen robes with siluer hemd:
> And on their heads with long locks comely kemd,
> They wore rich Mitres shaped like the Moone,
> To shew that *Isis* doth the Moone portend;
> Like as *Osyris* signifies the Sunne.
> For that they both like race in equall iustice runne.
>
> [vii. 3–4]

The Temple with its long-haired priests depicts an English court of law (Lerch, p. 102), yet one in which, strangely, Talus as the law has no place. René Graziani and Frank Kermode have suggested that the Temple represents the courts of royal prerogative—especially the Chancery—known as courts of equity and possessing the function of mitigating the rigor of the common law in cases where the provisions of the common law were unduly severe for the particular circumstances.[11] Yet it is overly restrictive to interpret Spenser's analysis of justice, as Kermode does, in terms of the historical competition for jurisdiction between the English courts of common law and equity, for the complementary relationship of law and equity was a commonplace of European legal theory.

As a kind of ideal justice, equity influenced the application of law in extenuating circumstances. This influence, in theory, could intensify as well as lessen the severity of the law, but, in practice, equity had normally a mitigating function. Jean Bodin explains its role as one of interpreting the intent and adjusting the force of the law in particular cases: "Equitie referred vnto a soueraigne prince, is as much as for him to declare or expound, or correct the law: but referred vnto a magistrate or iudge, is nothing else, but for him to asswage and mitigat the rigor of the law: or as occasion shall require aggrauat the too much lenitie thereof: or else to supply the defect thereof when as it hath not sufficiently prouided for the present case offered, that so the purport and meaning of the law saued, the health and welfare both of the lawes and commonweale may be respected and prouided for" (VI.vi, p. 763). Bodin makes clear that this mitigation or stiffening of rigor must not violate the essence of the law: "Howbeit yet . . . the magistrat must not so farre bend the law, as to breake the same, although that it seeme to be right hard" (VI.vi, p. 764). Lipsius warns, "Let him not violate the laws, *for in them doth consist the safegard of the citie,*" but also urges, "let him sometimes temper them, for it is not spoken in vaine, that *auncient writers were of opinion that the extremitie of the lawe, was meere iniustice*" (II.xi, p. 30). The mitigating role of equity had been part of Artegall's education by Astraea, who

> him taught to weigh both right and wrong
> In equall ballance with due recompence,
> And equitie to measure out along,
> According to the line of conscience,
> When so it needs with rigour to dispence.   [i.7]

In the Temple of Isis, however, and throughout the greater part of Book V—until the parts of justice have been assimilated into the complete conception appearing in Artegall at the end—Artegall represents untempered justice. The crocodile Osiris, identified later with Artegall (vii.22), is restrained by the goddess Isis after having devoured the flames and tempest (vii.15), symbolic of the civil disorders that threaten the state.

The concept of equity as a principle mitigating the severity of the law blends easily with the concept of clemency, and in Spenser's view the two are virtually synonymous. The priest who interprets Britomart's dream explains her relationship to Artegall—and that of equity to justice—as one of clemency to severity.

> For that same Crocodile *Osyris* is,
> That vnder *Isis* feete doth sleepe for euer:
> To shew that clemence oft in things amis,
> Restraines those sterne behests, and cruell doomes of his.
> [vii.22]

Bryskett associates equity and clemency in remarking of justice, "She tempereth with equitie (which may be termed a kind of clemency ioyned to iustice) things seuerely established by law, to the end that exact iustice may not proue to be exact wrong" (p. 249). Spenser's personification of equity and justice in Isis and Osiris has an analogue in Lipsius's association of equity—or clemency—with the moon, as complementary with the sun of justice. "I present now vnto our Prince *Clemencie*, the other light, which is as I may call it, the Moone of Empires. This goddesse, is milde and gracious, who doth mollifie, and temper matters, taketh away the hurtfull, rayseth vp them that fall, and runneth to preserue those, that throw themselues headlong into daunger. I know not how I should describe it in other words, then *to be a virtue of the mind, which with iudgement, enclineth from punishment, or reuenge to lenitie*" (II.xii, pp.

31–32). The relationship of justice and clemency is complementary, not antithetical: "I côfesse that this moone, goeth somtime a litle aside, frō this sharpe & piercing sunne of iustice: she goeth a side indeed, but goeth not away, & that by a by-path, not by a contrary way" (II.xii, p. 33). Radigund's description as a darkened winter moon (v. 12) indicates that her relationship with Artegall is a perversion of that intended for Britomart and Artegall as equity and justice. In Artegall's enslavement by Radigund, Spenser represents the overbearing of justice by a sentimental unwillingness to apply the proper force of the law to a condition requiring correction. Talus and Britomart, in their overthrow of Radigund, demonstrate the complementary function of law and equity or clemency. Talus proceeds forthrightly and vigorously to capture the city but is restrained in his slaughter by Britomart, who

> though reuengefull vow she did professe,
> Yet when she saw the heapes, which he did make,
> Of slaughtred carkasses, her heart did quake
> For very ruth, which did it almost riue,
> That she his fury willed him to slake: [vii.36]

The two parts of justice represented in Talus and Britomart are conjoined in Mercilla's court. Mercilla's scepter—"The sacred pledge of peace and clemencie"—and sword—rusty through disuse and positioned, like the Crocodile in the Temple of Isis, at the feet (ix.30)—are emblems of the proper relationship of clemency (or equity) and law in the administration of justice. During the trial of Duessa, Arthur, inclined toward inordinate pity, represents a sentimental equity or clemency. Artegall, rigidly fixed in his determination for mere justice, is like untempered law. Mercilla's judgment corrects both and defines the conception of justice toward which the allegory has been building and which Arthur and Artegall exemplify in the final episodes of Book V.[12] Seneca's *De clementia* provides a helpful gloss on Mercilla's reluctant execution of Duessa: "Good morals are established in the state and vice is wiped out if a prince is patient with vice, not as if he approved of it, but as if unwillingly and with great pain he had to resort to chastisement. The very mercifulness of the ruler makes men shrink from doing wrong; the punishment which a kindly man decrees seems all the more severe."[13] Barclay's *Mirrour of Good Maners* advises,

> in chastising be not to vengeable,
> Unmercifull and sharpe, as ioyning in thy rage,
> Of anothers ruine, confusion and damage.
> But punish as one pensiue, not willing but dolent,
> As both for to punishe constrayned to the same. [p. 33]

Mercilla's reluctant imposition of the sentence of death upon Duessa is not, for Spenser, hypocritical but rather in its manifestation of the twofold constraint of justice and clemency exemplifies the conception of ideal justice developed in the preceding cantos. In the last two cantos of Book V, Artegall's restraint of Talus's slaughter of the servants of Grantorto (xi.65; xii.8) shows that Artegall has learned the lesson of Mercilla's court and can himself henceforth exemplify the more comprehensive concept of justice.[14]

The assimilation of equity-clemency to justice in Book V anticipates the assimilation of courtesy to justice in Book VI. Calidore's words to Crudor define the relation of courtesy to justice in terms of the relation of mercy to what is "right and dew":

> For nothing is more blamefull to a knight,
> That court'sie doth as well as armes professe,
> How euer strong and fortunate in fight,
> Then the reproach of pride and cruelnesse.
> . . . .
> Who will not mercie vnto others shew,
> How can he mercy euer hope to haue?

To pay each with his owne is right and dew.
Yet since ye mercie now doe need to craue,
I will it graunt, your hopelesse life to saue.

[vi.i.41–42]¹⁵

In complementing justice absolute with mercy, Spenser has prepared for his complementing of justice with courtesy, for one of the meanings of courtesy in contradistinction to justice is that of mercy as opposed to severity. Erasmus had associated courtesy with clemency and kindred virtues in opposition to severity: "A good prince must therefore use every caution to prevent any possibility of lowering the affections of his subjects. . . . The affections of the populace are won by those characteristics which, in general, are farthest removed from tyranny. They are clemency, affability, fairness, courtesy, and kindliness."¹⁶

Of justice Bryskett remarks, "She setteth vs in the direct way to felicitie" (p. 248). In *The Faerie Queene* the direct way to civil felicity is the road to Mount Acidale, whose two stages are the quests of Artegall and Calidore. The vision of the Graces, like the destruction of the Bower of Bliss and the conquest of Amoret in the Temple of Venus, is the goal of both books of the pair and symbolizes the cumulative achievement of both patron knights. The establishment by Artegall of a commonwealth "well framed vpon honest and godly lawes" (the phrase is Bryskett's, p. 71) is fundamental to the emergence of social harmony through the inducement of eloquence and comely example. In Ireland local assemblies upon hills were notorious for outbreaks of civil disorder. In *A Vewe of the Present State of Irelande*, Irenaeus says, "Theare is a greate vse amongest the Irishe to make greate assemblies togeather vppon a Rathe or hill theare to parlye (as they saie) about matters and wrongs betwene Towneshipp and Towneshipp or one priuate person and another But well I wote and trewe it hathe bene often times approued that in these metinges manye mischiefs haue bene

bothe practised and wroughte ffor to them doe Comonlye
resorte all the scum of lose people wheare they liste which
else they Could not doe without suspicion or knowledge of
others" (*Variorum*, 9:128–29). Canto ix of Book VI presents
a place like those commonly frequented in Irena's "ragged
commonweale" by vicious assemblies transformed into an
emblem of harmonious order. The work of Artegall has been
the imposition of civil calm, the minimum condition for the
realization of Calidore's vision.

Calidore's share of Hercules' labors enables the image of
cosmic disorder in the Proem to Book V to be displaced by
the dance of the Graces on Mount Acidale. Aptekar points
out that the signs of the zodiac were associated by Renaissance mythographers with the victims of Hercules (p. 158).
The Hercules motif therefore was a means of representing
the work of Artegall and Calidore as bringing the terrestrial
into harmonious correspondence with the celestial.

> Looke how the Crowne, which *Ariadne* wore
> Vpon her yuory forehead that same day,
> That *Theseus* her vnto his bridale bore,
> When the bold *Centaures* made that bloudy fray
> With the fierce *Lapithes,* which did them dismay;
> Being now placed in the firmament,
> Through the bright heauen doth her beames display,
> And is vnto the starres an ornament,
> Which round about her moue in order excellent.
>
> Such was the beauty of this goodly band.   [x.13–14]

The collaboration of Hercules-Artegall and Hercules-
Calidore has enabled the order of earth to rival even that of
the heavens, in which, moreover, no trace of the celestial
aberrations mentioned in the Proem to Book V appears. The
apotheosis of the "fourth Mayd" as "another Grace" culminates the motif of ascent to the heavens begun in Book V
with the flight of Astraea and implicit in the traditional
ascents of Hercules and his victims. In the Book of Justice,

heaven, in the person of Astraea and her proxy Artegall and the "Angel-like" Mercilla, has descended to reform earth; in the Book of Courtesy, earth is shown, by means of the gifts of the Graces, rivaling the harmony of heaven. The instrument in both phases of restoration is Hercules, who, according to Natalis Conti, after defeating Geryon by force built an altar to the Graces (MacIntyre, p. 10).

In the movement of the Graces to the piping of Colin Clout, the poem symbolically enacts the allegorical meaning and function of Books V and VI. Spenser's ideal of civil life has gradually taken form in response to, and with the accompaniment of, the melody of his poetry. The piping of Colin Clout associates the poet's art in Books V and VI with the ancient symbols of the civilizing power of poetry: Orpheus's taming the savage race and Amphion's raising the walls of Thebes.[17] The cumulative thematic development of Books V and VI has climaxed in a splendid image of Renaissance faith in the capacity of poetry to raise the quality of human life in social, as well as personal, conduct. The evanescence of the vision signifies both the unfinished state of Calidore's quest and the extent to which the ideal of Books V and VI remained unrealized in the world of Spenser's England.

In Book V civilization pushes west; in Book VI it presses north: the two social frontiers of Elizabeth's kingdom. The westward direction of Artegall's quest is appropriate for several reasons. Hercules civilized the West. Ideal justice, according to Cicero, is "right reason in agreement with nature" (*De re publica,* III.xxii), and the path of reason in Plato is that of the sun (Dunseath, pp. 49; 70–71; 149, n. 7). Artegall, as justice, is associated, in his identification with Osiris, with the sun (v.vii.4). But it was especially appropriate in that Ireland lay to the west, and Ireland was a primitive, barbaric society in which rudimentary justice was just beginning to take hold. In Scotland, scene of Book VI (the brigands have been identified as Scottish borderers in *Variorum,* 6:256, and the region includes the territories of "the Prince of *Picteland*" and the "Lord of *Many Islands*," VI.xii.4), the royal authority had been firmly established; and, though predatory raids in the border country were still common, the chief remaining challenge to Elizabeth's administration was to win the affections of a subject people, inspiring loyalty to the Crown and generous feelings between clans and individual countrymen.

A cryptic incident in Book VI gives special emphasis to the social purpose implicit in the pairing of Books V and VI. Calepine's chase and defeat of the bear parallels on a lesser scale Calidore's pursuit and conquest of the Blatant Beast. His uncertain wandering after having killed the bear and rescued the infant suggests the rather fitful and tentative progression of civilization on the social frontiers of Elizabethan England:

> So hauing all his bands againe vptide,
> He with him thought backe to returne againe:
> But when he lookt about on euery syde,
> To weet which way were best to entertaine,
> To bring him to the place, where he would faine,
> He could no path nor tract of foot descry,
> Ne by inquirie learne, nor ghesse by ayme.
> For nought but woods and forrests farre and nye,
> That all about did close the compasse of his eye.
>
> Much was he then encombred, ne could tell
> Which way to take: now West he went a while,
> Then North; then neither, but as fortune fell.
>   [iv.24–25]

Calepine's bewildered movements reflect the exasperated view of many an Elizabethan as well as Spenser of Elizabeth's indecisive measures for reducing the borderlands by stern justice and mild courtesy to the harmonious social order of central England. Calepine's efforts represent the actual, as Calidore's the ideal, program of the English government to extend its pattern of civil life throughout the infant empire. As the author of *A Vewe of the Present State of Irelande* surveyed the uncivilized land of his jurisdiction, he saw "nought but woods and forrests farre and nye." Calepine's eventual discovery of a clearing produces nourishment for the babe and the promise of a glorious future for the house of Sir Bruin. The successive efforts and cumulative achievement of Artegall and Calidore offer the same hope for the ragged purlieu of Elizabethan civilization.

6 · *The Private-to-Public Movement*

The distinction between human and fairy knights divides the six books of *The Faerie Queene* into two groups: the odd-numbered books, whose virtues are championed by human knights, and the even-numbered books, whose virtues are championed by fairy knights. Rosamund Tuve has remarked that "the hero is not always the principle in action but a learner who thus comprehends what it is" (*Allegorical Imagery*, p. 126). It is evident to any reader of recent Spenser criticism that the careers of Red Cross, Britomart, and Artegall are the ones usually discussed in terms of character development—of a gradual, painful process of self-realization enabling them to fulfill the missions accepted by them at the beginning of their adventures in Fairyland and the roles prophesied for them on the completion of their assignments—whereas Guyon, Cambell and Triamond, and Calidore are generally regarded as bloodless, static heroes.[1] The human heroes of holiness, chastity, and justice possess an interior life of greater complexity than that of the fairy heroes of temperance, friendship, and courtesy, and their characters are more amenable to psychological analysis and their careers to treatment as educations. Whereas the human knight must be educated to his role, the fairy knight instinctively understands his proper behavior; and when he swerves, he need only be reminded of the conduct that is natural to him and be restored to his better self.[2] Guyon and Calidore, for example, are hardly more accomplished or mature in their virtues at the end of their quests than they were at the beginning, whereas Red Cross and Artegall

embody much more fully and satisfactorily at the completion of their missions the virtues with which they were
endowed at the beginning. The quests of the heroes of
Books I, III, and V have therefore an internal aspect—a
pattern of growing awareness and emerging compe-
tency—that is absent from the quests of the heroes of Books
II, IV, and VI.

This generic distinction between the odd- and the even-
numbered books is supported by the fact that the heroes of
Books I, III, and V are shown to be united by a special
instinctive affinity not shared by the others. Britomart, on
encountering Guyon, is provoked to combat. She subdues
him before concord between them is established (III.i.4–
12). On encountering the Red Cross knight, Britomart
immediately makes common cause with him against his
enemies (III.i.22). Though Britomart fights with Artegall,
as well as with Guyon, the conflict is not that of the virtues
they represent, for the fight occurs in Book IV as the central
example of the process of spiritual union. By Book V, where
Artegall is invested with his significance as the champion of
justice, Britomart and Artegall are closely united in soul.
Spenser has thus established a special bond between the
virtues of Books I, III, and V, uniting Holiness and Chastity
in a "friendly league of loue perpetuall" (III.iv.4) and Chastity and Justice by betrothal.

Although all virtues derive ultimately from heaven and
are thence planted by God in the garden of the mind
(VI.Pro.3–4), Spenser's treatment seems to follow the
medieval distinction between the infused and the acquired
virtues. The virtues of the odd-numbered books are infused
by heaven into the soul, whereas those of the even-
numbered books are acquired by earthly experience. For
example, the reader learns of holiness by vision in canto x of
Book I but is instructed (Guyon is entertained!) by history
in canto x of Book II. On approaching the Mount of
Contemplation, Red Cross is invited, as a "man of earth," to

behold a sight "That neuer yet was seene of Faeries sonne" (I.x.52). Though the fairy champion of Book VI is permitted to see the vision of the Graces, he does not understand it; and when he approaches to learn its meaning, it disappears. Calidore exclaims to Colin, "Right happy thou, that mayst them freely see," and queries, "But why when I them saw, fled they away from me?" Colin replies, "Not I so happy . . . / As thou vnhappy, which them thence didst chace . . . , / For being gone, none can them bring in place, / But whom they of them selues list so to grace" (VI.x.19–20). Evidently Calidore is prevented by inherent limitations from understanding and participating in the vision (though as a recapitulation of the thematic development of Books V and VI it appears in Book VI). The incident is an interesting inversion of the situation familiar in folklore of a human being's stumbling by accident upon the dance of the fairies and being excluded by his human nature from participation. The virtues championed by the fairy knights are natural and empirical, whereas those of the human knights are supernatural and intuitive.

Paradoxically, the intuitive virtues must be developed through a process of education by the human knights, whereas the acquired virtues are instinctively possessed and practiced by the fairy knights. The explanation is, of course, the existence of a moral struggle in the fallen natures of the human knights and the absence of such a struggle in the unfallen natures of the fairies, who serve as comparatively simple allegorical types of virtue and vice.[3] Courtesy, a quality the reader must acquire by experience and self-discipline (cf. "stubborn Turks and Tartars never train'd / To offices of tender courtesy," *Merchant of Venice*, IV.i.32–33), is possessed innately by Calidore, "In whom it seemes, that gentlenesse of spright / And manners mylde were planted naturall" (VI.i.2). On beholding with admiration the comeliness of young Sir Tristram, Calidore responds in spontaneous eloquence: "He burst into these words, as to him seemed good" (VI.ii.24). It is perhaps significant that Talus, invincible page of Artegall in Book V, is bestowed by divine gift upon the knight of justice, whereas the invincible page of Arthur in Book VI, the Salvage Man, is acquired by Arthur in the course of his travels.

The poem stresses the heavenly nature and origin of holiness, chastity, and justice. Red Cross is instructed in holiness by the celestial Coelia and the vision of the heavenly Jerusalem. In Book III Belphoebe and Amoret are represented as of heavenly birth, conceived by Chrysogonee from the rays of the sun. The poet apostrophizes the virtue of Book III, chaste affection, as of heavenly origin:

> Most sacred fire, that burnest mightily
> In liuing brests, ykindled first aboue,
> Emongst th'eternall spheres and lamping sky,
> And thence pourd into men, which men call Loue;
> . . . .
> Well did Antiquitie a God thee deeme,
> That ouer mortall minds hast so great might,
> To order them, as best to thee doth seeme,
> And all their actions to direct aright;
> The fatall purpose of diuine foresight,
> Thou doest effect in destined descents,
> Through deepe impression of thy secret might.
>
> [III.iii.1–2]

The phrase "pourd into men" identifies chastity as one of the virtues infused by heaven into the soul. Artegall, knight of justice, was trained for his role by the goddess Astraea, who gave him Chrysaor—the sword used by Jove himself against the Titans—and her iron groom, Talus, and then "Return'd to heauen, whence she deriu'd her race; / Where she hath now an euerlasting place" as Virgo with her scales (V.xi.9). At the beginning of canto vii the poet exclaims,

> Nought is on earth more sacred or diuine,
> That Gods and man doe equally adore,
> Then this same vertue, that doth right define:

> For th'heuens themselues, whence mortal men implore
> Right in their wrongs, are rul'd by righteous lore
> Of highest Ioue, who doth true iustice deale
> To his inferiour Gods, and euermore
> Therewith containes his heauenly Common-weale:
> The skill whereof to Princes hearts he doth reueale. [v.vii.1]

Justice, like chaste love, is an attribute of God and must be imparted to men inwardly by revelation.[4] The deification of justice, like love, by the ancient world is in keeping with its divine nature and origin.

> Well therefore did the antique world inuent,
> That Iustice was a God of soueraine grace,
> And altars vnto him, and temples lent,
> And heauenly honours in the highest place;
> Calling him great *Osyris*.   [v.vii.2]

The supernatural revelation of the identities of Red Cross, Britomart, and Artegall by means of vision at the Mount of Contemplation (i.x), Merlin's cave (iii.iii), and the Temple of Isis (v.vii) allegorically enacts the infusion of the virtues of holiness, chastity, and justice into the mind.

There are, on the other hand, no deities of temperance, friendship (except as friendship forms a part of the larger concept—involving the union of sexual opposites—of universal concord), and courtesy (the Graces are, strictly speaking, agencies, rather than embodiments, of courtesy). Medina, Alma, Cambina, Agape, and the Fourth Grace are not goddesses but inhabitants of Fairyland. Whereas the virtues of the odd-numbered books are characteristically epitomized by theophany (Coelia, Diana, Venus, Adonis, Cupid, Astraea), those of the even-numbered books are epitomized by apotheosis (Alma, Cambina, Agape, the Fourth Grace).[5] The distinction enforced by these differences of representation is between supernaturally infused and naturally acquired virtues.

In Aquinas's divison of the virtues, the infused virtues are those that produce rectitude with regard to a divine standard, whereas the acquired virtues are those "whereby man behaves well in respect of human affairs" (*Summa Theologica*, I–II, q. 64, art. 1). Holiness, chastity, and justice, in Spenser's treatment, accordingly consist of conformity to an absolute divine standard, whereas temperance, friendship, and courtesy consist of practical norms of behavior. The ethical basis is religious on the one hand and pragmatic on the other. Lerch compares the rules of manners and laws of arms in Book VI that may yield to expediency—such as Tristram's attacking a knight (canto ii) and Calidore's white lie (canto iii)—with the absolutes of Book V that may not be violated without dire consequences—for example, Artegall's deviation from justice out of pity for Radigund (canto v).[6] Perhaps something of this distinction is implied in Spenser's declared intention to fashion a knight in "vertuous and gentle discipline," "vertuous" indicating the infused absolutes and "gentle" the acquired psychological and social norms of conduct.

Fritz Caspari singles out, besides the Book of Justice, "also and in particular the second, fourth, and sixth books, with their respective themes of temperance, friendship, and courtesy," as "Spenser's restatement of humanistic doctrine."[7] In Cicero's view of society these virtues derive in causal sequence from right reason. Human nature, thought Cicero, displays "two basic characteristics—man's possession of reason on the one hand and his natural sociability on the other. In Cicero's view the latter was a consequence of the former. The participation of all men in the reasoning faculty draws them together into fellowship and communication. Because they reason they communicate."[8] Right reason prompts temperance (as the Palmer, Guyon), which forges the "band of vertuous mind" that is friendship.[9] Friendship, according to Aristotle, is the main bond of society (*Nicomachean Ethics*, VIII.iii.6; cf. "friendly offices that bynde," VI.x.23). Though justice is also one of the social virtues deriving, according to Cicero, from right reason, Spenser relates it, by its heavenly nature and origin, to the series beginning with holiness and chastity and consisting of conformity to a supernaturally revealed standard. The causal sequence of the virtues of the odd-numbered books is a progression from rectitude with regard to the divine standard in private character to rectitude in interpersonal and intrapersonal relationships.

In each pairing, then, we encounter a movement from a virtue whose moral reference is vertical and whose essential concern is conformity to a divine absolute to a virtue whose moral reference is horizontal and whose essential concern is with earthly harmony. The progression is from heaven to earth, from the invisible to the visible, and from a personal to a social context. Giamatti succinctly contrasts the quests of Books I and II in terms of the contemplative and active ideals of virtue: "In Book I, the greatest temptation was to Despair, to sin against the spirit. . . . In Book II, the great temptation is to indulge in goods of this world, in the material joys of wealth and possessions . . . or sexual pleasure. . . . Temperance is not, like Holiness, a contemplative ideal, but is rather an active, 'natural,' physical ideal. It is much less immediately concerned with the next world, and is much more obviously concerned with this one" (p. 247). A. C. Hamilton remarks that "Guyon comes to restore man not to his rightful place as a citizen of heaven as does Arthur [in Book I], but to its counterpart, his rightful place upon earth" ("Like Race to Runne," p. 334). Arthur in Book I rescues man's soul; in Book II, his body. Bryskett in treating temperance stresses its earthly commodity: "This vertue which is the meane in all actions, and a seemlinesse in all things appertaining to ciuill life, doth increase mans praise and cōmendations, multiplieth honor vpon him, lengtheneth his life, and lightneth the burthen of all his troubles: finally it so fashioneth a man, as whether he be alone or in company, whether he be in publike or in priuat, he neuer vndertaketh any thing but that which carieth withall reputation, dignitie & honor" (p. 222). Temperance is a virtue concerned with earthly standards and rewards of conduct—namely, physical and emotional health, social propriety, and honor.

In passing from Book III to Book IV, as Roche observes, we are alerted by "the carefully arranged pairs of riders" to a shift "from the concept of love in the individual to love as a social phenomenon" (p. 206). The action of Book III "imitates the interior and solitary battle of love within the individual"; that of Book IV, "the struggles of love in society" (p. 209). Amoret's adventures, as Mark Rose summarizes them, illustrate the personal-to-social progression of Books III and IV. Amoret in Book III, till freed by Britomart, is the solitary lover tormented by the fears and frustrations that arise within the mind during courtship. In Book IV "her injuries, received not only from Lust but also, inadvertently, from Timias, reflect the damage to her public reputation as a result of spending time with the monster and then being discovered in compromising circumstances with the squire. The wounds compel her . . . to take up a secluded existence in the woods. There, outcast from society, as if in fact a fallen woman, she lives in pain until the day when Arthur . . . comes to heal her and guide her safely through the House of Sclaunder" (p. 132). The suffering and separation of Amyas and Aemylia are, as we have seen, the consequences of putting personal desire before social considerations. The virtue of Book IV, in contrast to that of Book III, gives priority to social over personal obligations and is concerned chiefly with the effect of moral dereliction upon public reputation. Friendship, according to Bryskett, is a good in itself, but also and especially a social virtue "necessary for the accomplishment of ciuill felicitie, which without loue cannot be" (p. 225). Spenser's treatment of friendship completes a progression in the conception of love from a concern with personal integrity to a concern with social good.

The same progression appears in the last pair of books. Artegall, when assailed by Envy, Detraction, and the Blatant Beast, "past on, and seem'd of them to take no keepe" (v.xii.42), confident in the immunity afforded by his personal integrity. Social disapprobation is not a threat to virtue in Book V, where the proper administration of the virtue of justice requires an insensitivity to the opinions and feelings of others. Kathleen Williams, in her study of the fictional coherence of the quests, has emphasized the loneliness of the quest of Artegall: "Artegall's actions and the character he reveals through them are shaped by his isolation, and by his committal to an almost impossible task." After Astraea flees the earth, "he is left to act alone, one just man among many unjust" (*Spenser's World of Glass,* p. 156). The exercise of justice requires the denial of the claims of all human ties. Hurault recalls that "Plutarch sayth in the life of Aristides, that whensoeuer the case concerned iustice, friendship could beare no sway with Aristides, no not euen for his friends, nor enmitie prouoke him against his enemies" (p. 184). It is appropriate that the books of friendship and justice are the only books not provided with a link in *The Faerie Queene.*[10] In Book VI the chief threat to virtue is susceptibility not to evil influences but to social reprobation. The characters err not by deviation from an intuited standard of right but by reckless unconcern for the disapprobation of others. The bite of the Blatant Beast symbolizes, as J. C. Maxwell has observed, injury to reputation, not the attempt of an opposing vice "to establish itself in the human soul."[11] The context is social rather than personal.

In each pairing of books a private virtue is directed outward to public responsibility and honor. The relationship between the thematic concerns of the books is therefore cumulative, not antithetical or merely complementary. Holiness, in public conduct, is reflected in temperance; chaste affection, in enduring friendship (in both sexual and asexual relationships); justice, in its most comprehensive sense, in courtesy. The second virtue of each pair must be supported—indeed informed—by the first, just as the first virtue is necessarily fulfilled by the second. The virtues of Books II, IV, and VI are concerned with earthly harmony: within the mind, between friends, and among individuals in society. The characteristic action of the exemplars of each book is mediation, undertaken by Medina, Cambina, and Calidore, as well as Arthur in these books.[12] The book pairings imply a causal relation, in terrestrial as well as celestial order, between harmony and fidelity to divine decree. The harmony sought by the champions of temperance, friendship, and courtesy is a consequence of the rectitude that is the object of the quests of holiness, chastity, and justice. The quests in each pair are phases of a single action whose movement is resolutely toward public virtue.

This thrust from private to public virtue appears also in the relations of the three-book groupings that constituted the installments of publication. Charles G. Smith made the observation years ago that "in the first three books Spenser is interested in the virtue of the individual as such: his holiness, his temperance, his chastity—the harmony of the whole nature controlled by reason" but that "beginning with the fourth book he turns to a more definite study of the individual in relation to other individuals" (*Variorum*, 4:307). Thomas Roche and Northrop Frye have pointed out that holiness, temperance, and chastity, when compared as a group to friendship, justice, and courtesy, appear as personal or private virtues in relation to social or public virtues.[13] Frye regards this dichotomy as an abandonment of the "appalling spectre" of the twenty-four-book plan, in keeping with his view of the poem as complete in its present state. He suggests "a kind of Hegelian progression" within each group of books, in which the third virtue of each group is a synthesis of the preceding two. It may be more pertinent that in Christian thought holiness is the root of all personal virtue, just as in classical political theory friendship is the basis of society. The first three books, at any rate, are concerned with inward order; the last three, with outward order. The chief threat to the inward order of Books I, II, and III is illusion—the false dream—and, accordingly, the agents of disorder are evil magicians and enchantresses. The enemy of outward order in Books IV, V, and VI is selfish ambition, reckless of social responsibilities, asserted in such forms as defiance of parents in elopement, political tyranny, and (in its thwarted form) envy and slander. The agents of disorder in these latter books are monsters and tyrants. Atin embodies the inner disorder of the first set, Ate the external disorder of the second.

The progression from private to public in the three-book groupings is, as in the pairs of books, cumulative, with the earlier virtues participating in the latter. This relationship is especially evident in the books of the cardinal virtues temperance and justice. Spenser introduces Guyon into Book V at the marriage of Florimell and Marinell so as to communicate his virtue to Artegall.

> Much was the knight incenst with his lewd word,
> To haue reuenged that his villeny;
> And thrise did lay his hand vpon his sword,
> To haue him slaine, or dearely doen aby.
> But *Guyon* did his choler pacify,
> Saying, Sir knight, it would dishonour bee
> To you, that are our iudge of equity,
> To wreake your wrath on such a carle as hee:
> It's punishment enough, that all his shame doe see.
>
> So did he mitigate Sir *Artegall*.   [iii.36–37]

Dunseath observes that temperance is present in Mercilla's court (V.ix.32) and rightfully so since mercy was traditionally an aspect of temperance (p. 214). Actually the conception of justice as a harmony of all the faculties is almost identical with the virtue of temperance, and Spenser has already developed the personal aspect of justice in the allegory of Book II.[14] In Artegall the personal justice contributed by Guyon's achievement fuses with the public justice he gradually masters to perfection. In Book IV the union of Artegall and Britomart in betrothal exemplifies not only the spiritual bond of friendship but also the ideal of chaste affection in Book III. Something of the virtue of Book I seems implicit in the epithet "righteous Artegall" as well as in his immunity by reason of personal probity to the attack of Envy, Detraction, and the Blatant Beast. Calidore's winsomeness certainly owes something to his sense of moderation, the essence of temperance; for the soul of decorum is rational control and exercise of the faculties in relation to a given social situation. Fundamental to the success of the second set of quests are the achievements of Red Cross, Guyon, and Britomart in the first three books, and they pass on their essential traits to their allegorical descendants, the heroes of Books IV, V, and VI.

A consideration of the relations of the six-book groupings carries us, of course, into the realm of speculation; but if the hypothesis advanced in chapter 2 is correct, Spenser had two cardinal virtues left to form the keystones of the remaining three-book groupings as the subjects of Books VIII and XI. Although all four of the cardinal virtues were traditionally associated with the education of the ruler (Harris, pp. 145–52), the virtues of fortitude and prudence had a special place in determining fitness to rule. Since the publication of Robert Kaske's paper *"Sapientia et Fortitudo* as the Controlling Theme of *Beowulf"* (see chap. 3, n. 1), students of literature have recognized the importance of the complementary relationship of these virtues as an epic formula in Western literature. In Hoccleve's *De Regimine Principium* (written for the instruction of Henry, Prince of Wales, later

Henry V), they appear in complementary relation as virtues
necessary to the warrior-prince in the exercise of arms:

> O worthi Prince! I truste in ȝour manhode,
> Medlid wiþ prudence and discrecïoun,
> That ȝe schulle makë many a knyȝtly rode,
> An þe pride of oure foos thristen adoun.
> Manhode and witt conquéren hy renoun;
> And qwo-so lakkiþ outhir of þe tweyne,
> Of armës wantiþ þe bridel and reyne.
> . . . .
> Whan reueled wit and manly hardynesse
> Ben knytte to-gidre, as ȝok of mariage,
> Ther foloweþ of victorie þe swetnesse;
> ffor to sette on hym whettith his corage,
> And wit restreyne his wil can & aswage
> In tymë duë, and in couenáble;
> And thus tho two ioynt ben ful profitable.[15]

In a later work concerned with the preparation of young
Henry, the question of Prince Hal's fitness to rule is put
forth and resolved by Shakespeare in terms of these virtues.
Hal demonstrates his qualifications in rejecting examples of
spurious fortitude and prudence in Hotspur (who displays
courage and strength without prudence) and Falstaff (who
evinces prudence—"discretion"—without courage and
strength) and furthermore by exemplifying the genuine
virtues in his disengagement from his Boar's Head companions and his valor during the Battle of Shrewsbury. Eno-
barbus undercuts Antony's appearances of fortitude by
censuring his lack of wisdom:

> I see still
> A diminution in our captain's brain
> Restores his heart. When valour [preys on] reason,
> It eats the sword it fights with: I will seek
> Some way to leave him.   [III.xiii.192–201]

Fortitude and prudence had a unique status as mutually
defining and supporting virtues essential to the successful

exercise of both military and political leadership. Together they epitomized the heroic ideal inherited by Spenser's age. It appears, then, that Spenser's distribution of the cardinal virtues in the six-book dichotomy provides for the same progression from private to public virtue that we have observed to obtain on other structural levels of the poem.[16]

Arthur's quest for glory, though insufficient in the view of many critics to provide necessary unity to the fictional narrative, informs the allegory of *The Faerie Queene* and the system of virtues that expresses it. The complementary dichotomy of private and political virtues projected for the twenty-four-book scheme evidently was intended to comprise in the constituent structural dichotomies of the entire poem, just as in those of the existing fragment, a cumulative progression from private integrity to public demonstration and reward. The effect is that of a systolic movement from private to public virtue on every structural level of the poem above that of the single book, reinforcing the direction and impetus of Arthur's quest, and the reader's education, toward public responsibility and honor. This integration of theme into structure reflects the purpose of heroic poetry as defined by Sidney in the *Apology*: to bestow a hero upon the world. Spenser's ideal gentleman is, of course, not primarily an exemplar of military prowess but one who like Aeneas, in the interpretation of Virgil's poem familiar to Spenser, has conquered his own weaknesses and is ready to help shape the destiny of his country.

PART III

INTERLACING:
MULTIPLE EMBODIMENTS

Goodness doth not move by being, but by being apparent; and therefore many things are neglected which are most precious only because the value of them lieth hid.

Richard Hooker,
Of the Laws of Ecclesiastical Polity, i.vii

7 · *Variety and the Moral Dialectic*

One of the most frequent and telling, to modern sensibilities, of the censures of unsympathetic criticism of Spenser's poetic is the charge of redundancy. It is unlikely, however, that Renaissance readers of *The Faerie Queene* would have considered redundancy, at least in the sense of "variety," a blemish on Spenser's art.[1] In Muzio's *Arte Poetica* (1555) it is variety through which poetry performs its function of providing pleasure.[2] Spenser in the Letter to Raleigh explains that he has analyzed Arthur's virtue of magnificence into twelve other virtues, each with its own patron knight and its own quest, "for the more variety of the history." Unless Renaissance criticism was divorced from Renaissance sensibility and Spenser in the Letter to Raleigh greatly misgauged his readers' taste, his use of multiple embodiments was not incompatible with the aesthetic of the age, and he could expect his readers to respond favorably to copiousness and exuberancy of invention, providing of course that judgment, the faculty that guides creativity according to intention, remained in firm control. Indeed it is likely that the faculty of judgment would regard benignly a certain amount of repetition for the mere sake of emphasis, since in the tradition of rhetorical criticism inherited by the Renaissance repetition served the didactic, as well as the pleasurable, end of literature as an important means for the enforcement of doctrine. It is therefore quite understandable, if not altogether excusable by modern aesthetic criteria, that in the scale of values of a successful Renaissance poet the principle of repetition might well have surpassed in importance that of economy of means.

There is in fact an indication in the Letter to Raleigh that repetition is an important principle of development in *The Faerie Queene*. Having explained the twofold signification of Gloriana as glory in general and Elizabeth in particular, Spenser adds, "And yet in some places els, I doe otherwise shadow her. For considering she beareth two persons, the one of a most royall Queene or Empresse, the other of a most vertuous and beautifull Lady, this latter part in some places I doe express in Belphoebe." A single entity—Elizabeth or the ideal ruler—appears in different embodiments in such a way as to reveal its attributes. In the passage that follows, Spenser identifies Arthur as magnificence and the knights whose quests constitute the special concerns of the separate books as embodiments of the component virtues of magnificence. The knights, individually, reflect aspects of the virtue imaged in Arthur and, collectively, form a second, composite embodiment of that virtue. Evidently we may expect persons and conceptions to appear in more than one embodiment and their appearances to serve an allegorical rather than a purely fictional purpose.[3]

That the operation of this principle of development extends well beyond the instances mentioned in the Letter to Raleigh is clear from the appearance of other avatars of Elizabeth in the course of the poem: of Una, Britomart, Astraea, and Mercilla.[4] Having been alerted to the multiple appearances of Elizabeth and the analytical relationship of the patron knights to Arthur, the reader is prepared to notice, for example, chastity embodied not only in Britomart but also in the complementary figures of Belphoebe and Amoret as virginal and married chastity (Belphoebe, like Gloriana and many other of Spenser's characters, has thus a moral and historical identification), justice not only in Artegall but also in Talus and Britomart as law and equity, and courtesy not only in Calidore but also in

Calepine and the Salvage Man as courtly and natural courtesy. Thus informed, the reader will realize that just as the various reflections of Elizabeth accumulate into a total conception of her character and rule as idealized by her subjects, so the repetition of embodiments of a particular virtue takes on an incremental rather than a merely redundant significance. The examples of courtesy in Book VI—Tristram, Calepine, Salvage, and Meliboe—present partial, precisely related aspects of the total conception—the ideal—that the poem aims to convey. In the case of apparent duplications, the reader is prepared to look for degrees of realization in which the second example has been invested with the results of the intervening allegory and presents a more complete view of the emerging conception than the first. Alma's Castle, in relation to Medina's, offers a view of temperance as the harmonious arrangement of all the human faculties, rather than of just the irascible and concupiscible passions. Whether analytical or cumulative in their sequential relations, the poem's avatars are integrally involved in the allegorical definition of the virtues.

It appears therefore that although Spenser's use of avatars may seem to justify the approach to the unity of *The Faerie Queene* in terms of modern fiction, Spenser's sophistication is in traditional methods of development and modes of apprehension. Rosamund Tuve has associated Spenser's use of avatars with the medieval method of expounding the virtues in terms of their aspects or facets. Popular iconography assisted the learned treatise in pictorially representing moral abstractions in their attributes and operations (*Allegorical Imagery*, p. 73). Spenser's presentation of concepts through multiple and various embodiments, linked by pictorial resemblances with established iconographic meanings, is an outgrowth of this medieval mode of exposition.[5]

At this point it is necessary to distinguish between the general method of Spenser's moral allegory, which is the shadowing of universals in a variety of concrete particulars, and the more specific technique of associating through similarity of embodiment the particular manifestations as aspects of the universal they are bodying forth. Lucifera and Orgoglio are both examples of pride, but Orgoglio is not an avatar of the conception behind Lucifera in so precise a sense as is Philotime, whose similar description as a goddess of worldly fame invites the association of these temptresses as manifestations of worldly ambition: to Red Cross a species of pride, to Guyon a species of covetousness. The relationship between Lucifera and Philotime is established by the poem through pictorial and verbal resemblances, not simply left to be inferred from a similarity of the ideas behind the vehicles. It is in this stricter sense, in which multiple appearances are associated by similarity of embodiment, that avatars make their primary contribution as a structural principle in *The Faerie Queene*. On encountering a character or situation we sense that we have met that character or situation before. On reflection we associate its appearances as facets of a conception that is emerging in the poem. This is the sense in which avatars are explained in the Letter to Raleigh, for Spenser alerts the reader to recognize aspects of Elizabeth in the royal or divine virgin and of the principal virtues in the questing knight.

The examples just cited require a qualification, which introduces an important variation in Spenser's use of avatars for moral definition. If we ingenuously assume that every instance of a royal maiden and every appearance of a questing knight images ideal virtue, we shall be badly misled— as badly misled, in fact, as some of Spenser's characters. On the other hand, if we assume, with the equal ingenuousness of modern cynicism, that in Lucifera and Philotime, for example, Spenser is undercutting ironically the fame represented by Gloriana and her court (or that he has provided an ambiguous polarity of reference!), we shall err as far in the other direction. The truth is that definition by contrast within similarity is an important complement to definition by analytical and cumulative association in Spenser's moral dialectic. Furthermore, like the method of exposition by multiple and various manifestations, it has its origin in the expository method of traditional moral philosophy.

Rosamund Tuve has called attention to the prevalence of the practice in medieval moral treatises of pairing the virtues with their corresponding vices, ordinarily the seven spiritual virtues and the seven deadly sins.[6] This method of exposition is reflected in the words attributed to Spenser by Lodowyck Bryskett in *A Discourse of Civil Life: The Faerie Queene* is to be a work representing "all the moral virtues" by "assigning to euery vertue, a Knight to be the patron and defender of the same: in whose actions and feates of armes and chiualry, the operations of that vertue whereof he is the protector, are to be expressed, and the vices & unruly appetites that oppose themselues against the same, to be beate down & ouercome" (pp. 26–27). Implicit is a Prudentian conception of a struggle between good and evil in which a strict alignment of combatants by inherent contraries occurs and, moreover, in which a single virtue is opposed by a multiplicity of foes, for a virtue may have as many foes as it has facets or manifestations. Though Tuve has quite properly warned against reading *The Faerie Queene* merely as a psychomachia (since it offers a more subtle anatomy of the human character and depicts and enacts the complex process of a moral education in an alien world), the conception is still fundamental; the poem, as Lyle Glazier insists, presents us minimally with "the graph of Virtue and Vice."[7] The alignment of moral qualities is just as strict as that which appears in "The Parson's Tale" or as the underpinning of other of Chaucer's tales that are generally read for the enjoyment of the fiction.

Although the rich contribution of medieval allegory to the idea of the conflict between virtue and vice deserves emphasis, the definition of virtues by their corresponding vices derived from classical sources (Padelford, p. 334). In the *De inventione* Cicero distinguishes two ways in which vices are related to virtues: on the one hand are the vices that are the direct opposites of the virtues and on the other are "those qualities which seem akin and close to these but are really far removed from them. To illustrate, diffidence is the opposite of confidence, and is therefore a vice; temerity is not opposite to courage, but borders on it and is akin to it, and yet is a vice. In a similar way each virtue will be found to have a vice bordering upon it, either one to which a definite name has become attached, as temerity which borders on courage, or stubbornness which borders on perseverance, or superstition which is akin to religion; or one without any name. All of these as well as the opposites of good qualities will be classed among things to be avoided" (II.liv.165). Spenser had not yet treated fortitude as a major virtue, but Cicero's example of religion and superstition as apparent neighbors calls to mind Una's adventure in the house of Corceca, interpreted in the legend to the canto (I.iii) as "blind Deuotions mart." In the same canto in which true religion meets its "bordering vice" in Corceca as spurious faith, it meets its "opposite"—its overt and avowed enemy—in Sans Loy as rebellious irreligion.

We are now in a position to understand more precisely a fundamental organizing principle of Spenser's allegory. The abstraction to be defined is given an ideal embodiment or a series of partial embodiments of the ideal or both, but also one or more antitypes, which may take the form either of simple opposites or of counterfeits of the virtue being defined.[8] Gloriana's simple opposites are those mistresses that denounce virtue and reward evil: Abessa, Munera, and Briana, for example. Her counterfeits are those paramours and patronesses who reward their suitors with sorrow instead of joy and with shame instead of fame. In Books I and II her counterfeits as paramours are Duessa and Acrasia; as patronesses, Lucifera and Philotime, false goddesses of fame.[9] The quest of true earthly fame imaged in Arthur has for its opposite embodiments the sensual sloth of Mordant and Verdant in Book II and that of the Witch's Son in Book III. Arthur's morally inspiring and ennobling vision of Gloriana is opposed by the morally enervating vanities of inordinate affection; and his unremitting pursuit, by the lassitude of those entrapped by lust. Ironically Red Cross himself provides the example in Book I of an opposite to Arthur when, "Pourd out in loosenesse on the grassy grownd, / Both carelesse of his health, and of his fame," he gives himself over to the will of his enemies (vii.7). Its counterfeit (or perhaps "burlesque" would be more precise, since deception is hardly possible) is the boastful posturing of Braggadocchio, who assumes himself entitled to the reward without the rigors of a quest for honor and is entirely self-regarding in his efforts to advance himself.

The triad of essence (with its various aspects), opposite, and counterfeit is the basis of Spenser's definition of the virtues in the individual books of *The Faerie Queene*. After the linking episode, Britomart's first adventure is an encounter with her opposite, the lascivious Malecasta. The name *Malecasta* identifies her as the opposite of Britomart as chastity;[10] her other titles, the *Errant Damzell* and the *Lady of Delight,* reflect facets of her nature—infidelity and sensuality—that oppose the ideal of chastity. Spenser has already begun to distinguish his virtue of chastity from its counterfeit in the flight of Florimell from her would-be benefactors. He provides additional counterfeits in the unnatural sequestration of Marinell (III.vi) and Hellenore (III.ix—x). True chastity has nothing to do with a withdrawal or flight from eroticism prompted by irrational fear, materialism, pride, misogyny, or jealousy, or with involuntary abstinence. It is not, in Spenser, essentially a virtue of renunciation but the concomitant of an exclusive love. In Book VI the opposite of courtesy is imaged in Maleffort, the "proud, discourteous knight," Sir Turpine, and others, and in its extreme forms it expresses itself in cynically insolent and

deliberately provocative acts of aggression. Its counterfeit is
the vain, selfishly motivated courtliness that appears in the
relationships of Briana and Crudor and, especially, of
Mirabella and her suitors.[11]

Although the precise sense of avatars as recurring manifestations of essences excludes opposites and counterfeits,
they must be considered along with avatars as an important
part of Spenser's system of multiple embodiments. Here-
after, we will be concerned only with the elements of this
system that are linked by verbal or pictorial (that is, perceptual rather than merely conceptual) resemblances. The inclusion of only those opposites with an embodiment similar
to that of the virtue they oppose may seem to make the
distinction between opposite and counterfeit rather subtle.
It is not so in practice, however, for the opposite does not
masquerade as the essence, whereas the counterfeit does.
Geryoneo's shrine (v.x) is linked by similarity of embodiment with the Temple of Isis (v.vii). The idol above the
altar with the monstrous reptile underneath recalls the
statue of Isis with the crocodile under her feet (Lerch, p.
142; Aptekar, p. 151). But the overtly malicious purpose of
the shrine—as the lair of Geryoneo's monster, which de-
vours human sacrifices—makes deception as impossible as
it is unintended. As opposites they represent ideal and
vicious courts of justice, the one established for human
benefit, the other maintained for human exploitation.

The counterfeit possesses an embodiment intended to
create an illusion of the good it opposes, rather than simply
to pair it with that good as an opposite. Northrop Frye has
stressed the importance of the "symbolic parody" or "demonic counterpart" in the structure of the imagery (pp.
119ff). This feature conveys the impression of a perverse
creative force of immense energy, feverishly imitating every
manifestation of the good (MacLure, pp. 5–12). The arch-
counterfeit, the essence of falsehood itself, is of course
Duessa, who could "forge all colours, saue the trew"

(IV.i.18), just as the arch-counterfeiter is Archimago, whose name and character identify him as the father of all liars. Spenser's use of counterfeits is a reflection not only of Cicero's scheme of representing the virtues and vices but also of the commonplace of traditional moral philosophy that evil must win its adherents by impersonating good.

How can man voluntarily embrace vice (said M. *Dormer*) which of all things is the worst, since the same author saith, that al men couet what is good, and since without vertue there can be no good.

These two sayings (said I) are not contradictory: for the most wicked man aliue desireth what is good: and if vice should shew it selfe in his owne proper forme, he is so vgly and so horrible to behold, that euery man would flie from him: therefore knowing how deseruedly he should be hated and abhorred, if he were seene like himselfe, he presents himselfe vnder the shape of goodnesse, and hiding all his il fauoured face, deceiueth the sensitiue appetite; which being intised by the false image of goodnes, is so seduced, and through the corruption of his mind and iudgement, by the ill habit, contracted from his child hood, he embraceth that which (if his iudgement were soūd) he wold neuer do.

This exposition of Plato by Bryskett (p. 178), except for the humanistic doctrine of the predilection of reason for the good, accords with the warnings of the New Testament concerning the deceptiveness of evil. Since "Satan him self is transformed into an Angel of light . . . it is no great thing, thogh his ministers transforme them selues, as thogh they were the ministers of righteousnes" (2 Cor. 11:14–15). The conflict between essential and counterfeit virtue signals the struggle between good and evil at its fiercest and most fundamental point as the mutual antagonism of the true and the false, of reality and illusion. The counterfeit in Spenser's system links evil with falsehood in opposition to goodness and truth and shows both in irreconcilable conflict. Tertullian declares, "The Author of truth hates all the false; He regards as adultery all that is unreal. . . . He never will approve pretended loves, and wraths, and groans, and tears" (*De spectaculis,* xxiii; quoted by Spingarn, p. 5). As adulteration of and aberration from the truth, evil exists only in counter-relation to the good and, moreover, can only fabricate. Its fabricated forms are exposed and thereby destroyed by the appearance of the genuine, for the light of truth robs them of that pretense which is their essence. When the true Florimell could not be distinguished from the false,

> Then did he [Artegall] set her by that snowy one,
> Like the true saint beside the image set,
> Of both their beauties to make paragone,
> And triall, whether should the honor get.
> Streight way so soone as both together met,
> Th'enchaunted Damzell vanisht into nought:
> Her snowy substance melted as with heat,
> Ne of that goodly hew remayned ought,
> But th'emptie girdle, which about her wast was wrought.
>
> [v.iii.24]

Artegall's method of discerning is a basic method of disarming and defeating vice in *The Faerie Queene* that complements that of the direct clash of opposites in which the ugliness of vice appears openly and immediately in contrast to the beauty of virtue. In bringing into confrontation his avatars and pseudoavatars Spenser is engaged not only in the definition of the good by its distinction from the false but also in the exorcising of the false by its juxtaposition with the true. It is thus that we are to understand the double identities of Venus, Adonis, and Cupid (e.g., in the tapestries of the Castle Joyeous, III.i.34–38, and in the Garden of Adonis, III.vi) and of Genius (II.xii.46–49; III.vi.31–33), and impersonations such as Duessa's of Fidessa (I.ii.26) and Archimago's of a hermit (I.i.34) in relation to the appearance of the genuine in Una and the hermit Contemplation (I.x).

The exorcism of the counterfeit by juxtaposition with the

genuine appears not only in the confrontation of characters but also in the paralleling of situations in such a way as to point up their essential differences and thereby to distinguish between the concepts they represent. Artegall's yielding to Radigund (v.v. 11–16) is described in such a way as to recall his previous submission to Britomart (IV.vi. 19–23). In both situations, as he is about to administer the death stroke, the beauty of his antagonist, previously concealed by the helmet, causes him to swerve from his purpose and submit to her mercy. In the symbolism of the Temple of Isis (explained by the priest, v.vii. 21–22) Artegall's submission to Britomart is reinterpreted in the context of Book V as picturing the proper relationship between law and equity. It contrasts with his present ignoble subjection to Radigund (v.v–vii), whose Amazonian rule exemplifies the subversion of the natural hierarchy of the sexes and of the faculties of the mind (uxoriousness also occurs when the passions are permitted to dominate the reason).[12] The apparent similarity of the situations emphasizes their essential difference. In courtship the lover must be submissive, not coercive, toward his intended spouse, and the roles of the lovers are clearly differentiated according to sex. Accordingly, in Spenser's analysis of justice, the law must be interpreted with reference to equity, or ideal justice; and human law must acknowledge its inferiority to, as a fallible expression of, the principles of justice revealed to the reason. In the administration of justice, however, the law must be applied without respect to the sex of the offender. Spenser is defining true justice by distinguishing it from spurious justice and is exorcising the spurious by juxtaposing it with the genuine. By paralleling situations exemplifying the rule of equity and the rule of sentimentality—the rational regard for the principles of ideal justice and the irrational indulgence of human feelings—the poem reveals the essential difference within the apparent similarity. In doing so, it exposes and drives out the "demonic counterpart" that too easily may be mistaken for the genuine.

The strategy of composition illustrated above is obviously instrumental to the moral purpose indicated in the Letter to Raleigh. It informs the unfolding of the announced themes of the books. It brings narrative rhythm into the service of logical definition and rhetorical emphasis. Whether a strategy susceptible to so simple an analysis of relationships as has been undertaken in this chapter can be considered relevant to the success of a work of such rich complexity as *The Faerie Queene* depends somewhat upon the particular qualities for which the work is appreciated. Nevertheless it is the strategy, not its execution, that is simple. To appreciate its potentialities one has only to think of the diagrammatic arrangement of characters and situations in *King Lear*. The motivation of the action of the play is simple—and mysterious—enough to be furnished by a "graph of Virtue and Vice." In accounting for his violent anger toward Oswald, Kent need only say, "No contraries hold more antipathy / Than I and such a knave" (II.ii.93–94). In *The Faerie Queene*, as in *King Lear*, a set of moral contraries is reflected in a system of relationships between characters and between situations whose articulations are subtle and complex. As a feature of the poem in which are fused both its didactic and aesthetic intentions and which provides structural support in both schematic and organic modes of coherence, avatars furnish a point at which Renaissance and twentieth-century sensibility can unite in an appreciation of Spenser's achievement.

8 · *Avatars*

The conceptions underlying the allegorical imagery of *The Faerie Queene*, like the other components of Spenser's cosmos, through changes in form "their being doe dilate" (*Cantos of Mutabilitie*, vii.58). The root ideas through a succession of embodiments gain both precision and amplitude. The repetition therefore is not redundant but instrumental in the definition of the virtues. Simultaneously, it supports the unity of the poem by providing a structure of correspondences supplementary to that of the scheme of the quests.

A consideration of Spenser's use of avatars requires a precise definition and judicious application of the concept if it is not to merge on the one side with thematic representation and on the other with symbolic motif. Avatars, as distinct from thematic examples, are a form of symbolic reappearance in which the basis of recognition is perceptual rather than conceptual. A resemblance between vehicles of concepts induces a recognition of identity between the concepts themselves. As distinct from the particulars of a symbolic motif, avatars are agents of narrative—situations or characters—whereas a symbolic motif may consist simply of figurative embellishment. Avatars are necessarily involved with plot. Although they are a form of thematic representation and may participate in a symbolic motif, they do not share their essentially allegorical nature with these other modes of fictional coherence.

By this definition, though the behavior of the Salvage Man and the discovery of Pastorella's identity both exemplify concealed courtesy, they cannot be considered avatars of this idea, since their relationship is conceptual rather than perceptual. The appearances of flowers in relation to the idea of courtesy in Book VI are not avatars but rather a symbolic motif, for the appearances are, with the exception of Pastorella's birthmark (xii.18), not agents of narrative (Pro.4; ii.35; x.44; cf. v.xii.13). On the other hand, the role of the Salvage Man as an invincible page links him to Talus as an avatar of the force of a civilizing principle backed by heavenly sanctions. The recognition of their relationship is perceptual. The recurrence of the encircling dance in Book VI may properly be regarded as an avatar, as well as part of a symbolic motif, for its appearances are agents of narrative and not merely figurative embellishment or enhancement. The situation in which a beautiful maiden is elevated above and encircled by admirers, who entertain her with music, appears in the scene of the honoring of Pastorella by the shepherds and country lasses (ix.8—9) and reappears in the dance of the Graces around the Fourth Grace (x.11—12). The lady on the summit of the hill, the concentric circles of persons honoring her, the piping of the shepherds—these features of resemblance link the situations as appearances of the same concept (though with significant variations), which Spenser interprets as the harmony of courtesy (x.11—15).[1] The cacophonous swarming of the savages around Serena (viii.39—40) is obviously an antitype. In contrast the allusion to Ariadne's Crown (x.13), while adding another circle to the symbolic motif, does not add another avatar; for the image of the heavenly order is not, like that of the earthly, an agent of narrative. These distinctions may seem oversubtle, but they are necessary if one is to understand the special contribution of avatars to the unity of *The Faerie Queene.*

This contribution is an interlacing action that reinforces but also crosses other structures of coherence. Fundamental to the main framework revealed in the Letter to Raleigh is the avatar of the questing knight. It combines with a second avatar of character discussed in the Letter, the royal or divine virgin, to form a third avatar, the love quest. This avatar of situation provides fictional and allegorical relations that cross the formal divisions of the main framework. The various love quests of the poem interlock in such a way as to form a system working independently of, yet in harmony with, that of the quests ordained by Gloriana. Arthur's quest for Gloriana, as a quest for virtue comprising the twelve quests of the titular knights and as the love quest that comprehends all the other love quests, is the bond between the two systems.[2]

The love quests are related to the quest of Arthur for Gloriana and to one another in an autonomous system of avatars. Those involving Una, Belphoebe, and Britomart are linked directly with Arthur's quest for Gloriana in the identities of the female lovers as avatars of Elizabeth. To the quests involving these avatars of Elizabeth may be added that of Florimell, whose beauty Arthur mistakes for, or rather recognizes as, that ideal beauty which is an attribute of Gloriana (III.iv.45). These quests for, or by, the virtues of Elizabeth are associated with one another not only by their relation to this common allegorical center but also by additional correspondences. Belphoebe and Britomart are specially related as avatars of chastity, and their quests show the resistive and assertive aspects of the most distinctive virtue of Elizabeth's ideal private character. Their relationship serves also to tie into the system rooted in the avatars of Elizabeth the quest of Belphoebe's twin, Amoret; the daughters of Chrysogonee, in Book III, are complementary avatars of the married and virginal chastity that is imaged singly in Britomart. Moreover, just as the career of Britomart will combine the versions of chastity imaged in Belphoebe and Amoret, so Amoret's adventures are a composite of Belphoebe's and Britomart's in involving quests both for and by an exemplar of chastity ("by" to the extent Amoret carries her earlier signification of married chastity into Book IV, where Scudamour's quest for Amoret becomes a quest by Amoret for Scudamour). As the quest of a female for a male lover, Amoret's quest for Scudamour in Book IV is related not only to Britomart's for Artegall but also to Una's for Red Cross and to Florimell's for Marinell. With the exception of Una's quest for Red Cross, all of these love quests cross the formal divisions of the poem, and with Una's they form a structure of relationships spanning Books I to V that complements that of the scheme of the virtues. As an avatar of moral aspiration the love quest images that desire which must inform the experience of the reader in Fairyland—which indeed must cross the formal divisions of the poem—if he is to realize in his character the virtues objectified in the quests that form the main framework.

The fact that there are conceptual ligatures within the system of the love quests—the association of the quests involving Britomart, Belphoebe, and Amoret by what they represent rather than initially by special similarity of embodiment—does not vitiate the principle of perceptual recognition in the definition given previously or in these examples; for these conceptual links are simply clustering mechanisms within the total system, which is based on the perception of similarity of embodiment between instances of the royal or divine maiden and of the love quest. In fact part of the total system of the love quests is their conceptual alignment in opposition to another set of avatars. Whereas instances of the fulfilled, or ultimately to be fulfilled, love quest represent the realization of moral aspiration, images of failure appear frequently throughout *The Faerie Queene* representing its opposite. We meet recurrently a winsomely featured youth languishing from the consequences of a misdirected, thwarted, inhibited, or improperly controlled affection. The physical description of Mordant combines the impressions of exceptional but wasted possibilities:

> His ruddie lips did smile, and rosy red
> Did paint his chearefull cheekes, yet being ded,

> Seemd to haue beene a goodly personage,
> Now in his freshest flowre of lustie hed,
> Fit to inflame faire Lady with loues rage,
> But that fiers fate did crop the blossome of his age. [II.i.41]

The pity of his case, we are told, is that he might have succeeded in love. Similar images of the abortive quest, some of temporary and some of terminal failure, appear in the cases of Sir Terwin (I.ix.27–30), Phedon (II.iv.3–36), Verdant (II.xii.79–80), the Squire of Dames (III.vii.37–52), Scudamour (III.xi.7–20), Amyas (IV.viii.50–ix.9), Sir Terpine (V.iv.22–32, v.18), and Calepine (VI.iii.20–iv.2). (Sir Terpine and Calepine are less obvious examples; Terpine's plight is a consequence of Radigund's thwarted love, and Calepine's derives ultimately from his careless dalliance with Serena.) These images of abortive love quests parallel antithetically those of successfully sustained love quests, emphasizing as avatars of failure the importance of discernment and constancy in moral aspiration.

Another antitype of the love quest, which contrasts the quality rather than the persistency of the quests, inverts the terms of the pursuit of love: the chase by lust. Florimell's pursuit by the Foul Foster (III.i) and by the Witch's Beast (III.vii), the Squire of Dames's by Argante (III.vii), the nameless youth's by Ollyphant (III.xi), and Placidas's by Corflambo (IV.viii) image an unworthy obsession that competes with moral aspiration and disables the mind for moral achievement and honor. The escapes of Florimell represent its failure to pervert an exemplar, as well as an object, of ideal aspiration. The rescues of the Squire of Dames, the nameless youth, and Placidas, as well as Amyas, show its near success with less ethereal material. The avatars of the impaired and perverse quests perform, in collaboration with the avatars of success, the aesthetic function of interlacing diverse elements of the poem in an important secondary system of relationships.

The preceding analysis has been based on the association of images through the recognition of rather general resemblances, perhaps to the point of straining the credibility of the principle of avatars. It is true that a narrative as long as that of *The Faerie Queene,* especially one utilizing certain standard romance motifs, is bound to include some repetition; and therefore an attempt to demonstrate a meaningful pattern of repetition that confines itself to only the more general features of character and situation may not be very convincing. Still, the avatars of the questing knight, the royal or divine maiden, and the love quest are sufficiently well established by Spenser's explanation in the Letter to Raleigh and by obvious implication elsewhere to make the significance of their recurrence unmistakable. Furthermore, the more fundamental a conception is in the poem and, concomitantly, the higher its degree of abstraction and the more extensive its set of manifestations, the less concrete will be the features on which is based the recognition of similarity between its embodiments. There is a gradation of abstraction of the shared features according to the comprehensiveness of the conception. Avatars of fundamental essences are linked less concretely than avatars of particular aspects of essences that are more restrictive in their signification. The shared features of the serpent creatures—of Errour, Duessa's beast, the Dragon, and Geryoneo's monster—are less numerous and less concrete (though the individual examples are presented in considerable detail) than those of the reviling hags, who as manifestations of an aspect rather than of the essence of evil are less comprehensive in the scope of their reference. The common features of the serpents are only very general, befitting the comprehensiveness of the concept they represent, whereas the common features of the reviling hags present a quite concrete and precisely delineated image. The effect of this gradation is that of an Aristotelian deductive hierarchy of concepts in which the higher levels have a more general basis of classification than the lower. The difference between the form of Spenser's and of Aristotle's or Aquinas's or Bryskett's presentation of the virtues is that Spenser's system, besides being less rigorous, is revealed inductively through the perception of relationships between the embodiments of concepts.

We are now prepared to consider the extensiveness and density of the articulations of this system in relation to the particular episodes of the poem. On examining individual segments of narrative and tracing their connections, we encounter an intricate network of specific relationships, the complexity of whose articulations suggests a neurological analogy. An episode or the appearance of a character can function as an avatar in as many ways and on as many allegorical levels as it has facets of identity, and it can have as many facets of identity as it has conspicuous features able to carry conceptual significance. Belphoebe we know from Spenser's explanation in the Letter to Raleigh to be an avatar of Elizabeth's moral character. However, from her appearances in Book III we infer for her also the identity of virginal chastity. As virginal chastity Belphoebe images a concept less comprehensive than that of the moral character of the Queen. Indeed her signification is more limited than Britomart's, for it requires the complementation of married chastity, shown in Amoret, to fill out the idea of chastity imaged in Britomart. Thus, in a general, rather abstract sense, she complements Gloriana as an avatar of the Queen's moral character while in a specific, more concrete sense (she and Amoret are linked as twins) she complements Amoret as an avatar of one of the virtues that compose the Queen's moral character. Her two facets of identity give her the function of an avatar on two allegorical levels of the poem. Similarly, almost every major character and episode possesses multiple facets of identity; and each facet, as a single image in a series of appearances of the concept or aspect it reflects, links the character or episode to which it belongs with others throughout the poem.

The defeat of Red Cross by Orgoglio demonstrates the complexity and extensiveness of connections of the avatars clustered in a single episode. Having escaped from the Palace of Lucifera, Red Cross is overtaken by Duessa as he is resting beside a fountain, his armor off and his steed foraging nearby. He engages her in lascivious play and drinks from a fountain, whose waters so debilitate him that he is helpless to resist the assault of Orgoglio.[3] The giant throws him into a dungeon within his castle and takes Duessa as his mistress, giving her a seven-headed reptile to ride. The dwarf flees with his master's armor to find help.

The case of Red Cross at the beginning of the episode is in its general contours a repetition of the Fradubio story (i.ii), in which the unfortunate knight, having been deceived into abandoning his proper love, wins as a martial prize and takes as his mistress a witch intent on his ruin. His lustful dalliance with Duessa enacts his illusions of Una's lewd advances and of her infidelity with the young squire (i.i–ii). The irony of the failure of Red Cross to recognize in his own experience the reappearance of Fradubio's and of the image of wantonness and infidelity that had incensed him against Una should impress upon the reader not only the frailty of human flesh but also the importance of the repetition of situations by Spenser. His repetition is the result of an inventive, rather than of an unproductive, imagination. The strictures of critics concerning Spenser's redundancy make it amply evident that there is critical, as well as moral, peril in the imperception of Spenser's avatars.

The image of the unarmed knight, diverting himself in the shade with his mistress, lulled by the murmuring waters of a brook or fountain and by the caroling of the birds, recurs in the prostrate figures of Cymochles and Verdant in Book II (vi. 13–18; xii. 70–80) and, without the brook or the birds, of Aladine and Calepine in Book VI (ii. 16–18; iii. 20). As an avatar of the relaxed will, it is an antitype of Arthur's vision of Gloriana, which, conversely, inflamed Arthur with a will to virtue (I.ix.12–14). The reference to the greenness of the boughs recalls the color of Lechery in the procession of the Seven Deadly Sins—"in a greene gowne he clothed was full faire" (I.iv.25)—and anticipates the settings of the Bower of Bliss and Malecasta's Castle, both of which are approached by a spacious plain that is, like Lechery, "Mantled with greene" (II.xii.50; III.i.20).[4] The conjunction of greenness and gloomy shade—"And with greene boughes decking a gloomy glade"—associates the bright allurement and dark consequences of lascivious pleasure. The "gloomy glade" requires "decking" with "greene boughes" in order to disguise the gloom of its shadows. These elements of Red Cross's experience are represented separately in Book II by Verdant and Mordant, whose physical surroundings as well as names and circumstances reflect stages of the temptation by Lechery. Verdant is encountered by Guyon in an earthly paradise (II.xii) and Mordant, dead, in a dark thicket within a wood (II.i.35–41). In Red Cross's experience Verdant very nearly becomes absolute Mordant; the greenness, by the time of Arthur's intervention, has already become gloom.[5]

Orgoglio's entrance is the first appearance of the giant in *The Faerie Queene*. His bulk links him with Argante (III.vii), Ollyphant (III.xi), Corflambo (IV.viii), the Egalitarian Giant (V.ii), and Disdain (VI.vii.41–44). The special emphasis upon his towering, scornful carriage and the attribution of a common parentage (VI.vii.41) link him particularly with Disdain. Thus linked, Orgoglio and Disdain image pride in two contexts: the one, the spiritual pride that is the mortal enemy of holiness, and the other, the pride of birth and natural gifts that is the mortal enemy of true courtesy. The imprisonment of Red Cross by Orgoglio anticipates the reported practice of Argante (III.vii.50) and the imprisonment of Amyas by Corflambo (IV.viii). Both Red Cross and Amyas are left to languish in a giant's dungeon because of ill-advised love.

Giantism in *The Faerie Queene* signifies the hypertrophy of a vicious passion into a monstrous travesty of the virtue it opposes. Dwarfism signifies the subordination of reason either properly to the suprarational, as to Una in Book I, or improperly to the infrarational, as to Corflambo in Book IV, in a servile role. Reason can render valuable service to holiness, but it can serve carnal impulses as well. Spenser's dwarfs characteristically follow their masters or mistresses and perform inconspicuous but necessary service. They normally are shown attempting to aid or impede the escape from vice. Corflambo's dwarf, a jailer (IV.viii.54), is an instrument of captivity rather than of escape. Placidas's kidnapping of and flight with the reluctant dwarf on horseback from the pursuing Corflambo inverts the situations of the previous appearances of the dwarf, in which he flees (I.vii) or pursues (III.v) on foot to find help for his imprisoned master or mistress. Through the association of two avatars and an antitype of servile reason, Spenser shows that a perversely subservient reason impedes, just as a properly subordinate reason aids, the escape from an enslaving vice.

The seven-headed beast of Duessa is one of many serpent creatures in the poem that image in their common features essential evil. When one meets such a creature as Duessa's beast, he is supposed to associate it with the other serpents—with Errour (I.i), the dragon beneath Lucifera's feet (I.iv.10), the dragon slain by Red Cross (I.xi), the dragon beneath the feet of blind Cupid (III.xi.48), and Geryoneo's monster (V.xi)—as various appearances of the same evil principle. The image and its reference derive from both biblical and classical sources: from the serpent in Genesis, Leviathan in Job, and the seven-headed beast and the dragon in Revelation, and also from Typhon and Echidna, the great primeval serpents, male and female, who battled the gods and begot monstrous forms of evil.[6] The description of Duessa's beast associates it implicitly with the seven-headed beast of Revelation and explicitly with the hydra destroyed by Hercules. Renaissance mythography associated the figures of pagan mythology with their supposed counterparts in the Scriptures as appearances, though somewhat blurred and partial, of the one eternal truth. Spenser's use of avatars is in accord with what appeared to be the method of divine revelation. In linking his incidents to one another, Spenser was imaging in them eternal truths in a manner in which Infinite Wisdom had revealed fragmentary truth to the ancients. In the Scriptures themselves Spenser could find inspired examples of such avatars as the serpent, the garden, and the sacred mount.

Of the score or so incidents cited as connected by avatars to the episode of Red Cross's defeat by Orgoglio, each is itself a complex of avatars referring to characters and episodes throughout the poem. For example, in the Disdain episode (VI.vii) Mirabella's mistreatment is a composite image of earlier instances of the humiliating affliction of a woman: of the dragging of the Squire's lady by Maleffort (VI.i.17), of the driving of the lady on foot by the mounted Discourteous Knight (VI.ii.10), and of the leading of the wounded Serena by Calepine as a consequence of the discourtesy of Sir Turpine (VI.iii.46). Mirabella is "Vpon a mangy iade vnmeetely set" with "a lewd foole her leading thorough dry and wet" (VI.vi.16). Led by Disdain and driven by Scorn, Mirabella images both the extremity of discourtesy and the truth that those injured by discourtesy generally have made themselves vulnerable by insensitivity toward others and unconcern for their reputation. The picture of the subdued Timias, bound and led on a leash, inverts Satyrane's binding and leading of the Witch's Beast with Florimell's girdle (III.vii.36) and Calidore's of the Blatant Beast (VI.xii.34–37), of which it is an antitype. Arthur's rescue of his helpless Squire from the affliction of Scorn recalls his earlier rescue of Timias from the associate of a giant, when Timias was overcome by Duessa and her beast (I.viii). Finally, Mirabella's restraint of Arthur and the

Salvage Man from destroying Disdain and Scorn (VI.viii. 17) lest her life by their deaths "haue lamentable end" recalls Amoret's similar restraint of Britomart from destroying her tormentor, Busirane, lest "her paine / Should be re-medilesse, sith none but hee, / Which wrought it, could the same recure againe" (III.xii.34).

The interconnection of the episodes by avatars forms an extensive network of relationships that provides allegorical, as well as fictional, coherence. In their clustering of images, successive episodes continually draw together elements from various parts of the preceding narrative into new combinations with new relationships and give them a renewed life with additional accretions of meaning. They may also supply new images and initiate their careers as avatars. In the episode that follows the one just discussed, the blindness and senility of Ignaro join the attributes of blindness and ignorance already encountered in Corceca and Abessa (I.iii), and his backward face anticipates the same indication of fear and indirection in the fleeing Trevisan (I.ix.21) and Florimell (III.i.16). The darkened, debilitated mind of the worshiper is revealed in the custodian of her religious mysteries; and his timorousness, in turn, appears later as a consequence of despair and the cause of a mistaken (in her flight from Arthur) and spurious chastity. The effect of the articulations of the system of avatars is thus a continuing enrichment, refinement, and consolidation, in various ways, of the accumulating meanings of the allegory. Each episode and indeed each avatar makes its own contribution both to the density of the texture of the allegory and to the dynamism of its movement toward Cleopolis.[7]

9 · *Counterpoint and Counterfeit*

Antitypes are a variation of avatars in their linking of concepts by similarity of embodiment but are distinguished from true avatars in that the concepts are opposites rather than aspects of a single idea. Like avatars of essences, antitypes may be of character or situation.[1] For example, the triple force of Geryoneo (v.xi) recalls that of Triamond (IV.iii), though his dishonorable purpose identifies the concept he represents as opposite to that of Triamond (Aptekar, pp. 147–50). As female rulers or would-be rulers whose power is challenged by force, Radigund and Duessa (in v.ix) are counterparts of Belge and Irena, but they contrast as opposites in their character as usurpers and in their readiness to take advantage of sentimental, rather than of true, justice. The youths Amidas and Bracidas (v.iv) recall by the circumstance of the similarity of their names Amyas and Placidas (IV.viii), but the discord between the two brothers is meant to contrast with the concord between the two friends (Lerch, p. 83). A character or situation may have more than one antitype. The Temple of Venus episode (IV.x) includes among its antitypes the perilous bridge of Pollente (v.ii) and the island fortress of the brigands (VI.x–xi), both of which reflect forms of discord in society. Conversely a character or situation functioning as an antitype may oppose more than one avatar of virtue. Radigund, imaging the tyranny of the female over the male, of passion over reason, and of false over true justice, is an antitype of Britomart in at least two different ways and of Mercilla also. Duessa opposes numerous concepts of virtue (e.g., faith, true religion, concord, just rule) in the course of her career. A character or situation thus can be opposed by as many antitypes or can function as an antitype in as many ways as it has facets of identity. The consequence of multiple opposition is the addition of another system of complex relationships to that of the multiple embodiment of essences.

Furthermore avatar and antitype not only exist in single opposition but also and often participate in counterpointed series of avatars of virtue and vice. In fact the most striking contribution of antitypes to the unity of the poem is in the insistent antithetical parallelism of similar embodiments of virtue and vice. Certain general features of the allegorical landscape serve as vehicles for associating various forms of virtue and vice in sustained opposition as aspects of the single moral opposition underlying the thought of the poem. Though not all castles, for example, are described in such detail as to make them precise allegorical embodiments of a concept, all represent to some degree strongholds of virtue or vice. When a character approaches a castle, we regard it as boding good or evil to him. The good or evil it bodes and eventually brings to him, whether objectified in the description of the castle and its inhabitants or generally exemplified in the treatment of the knight, is pertinent to the concerns of the particular book in which the castle appears. In a particular book, castles of virtue and vice appear in general, if not specific, opposition, and they are frequently linked specifically as avatars or antitypes with castles in other books. It is, however, the general arrangement of castles in opposing ranks throughout the books that supports the impression of the poem as a unity by reinforcing the concept of the unity of the virtues (cf. 1.ix.i) and the solidarity of the vices whose domains are defined by the book divisions, and simply by contributing a conspicuous pattern of recurrence.

The rescue of Red Cross by Arthur (1.viii) offers a convenient collocation of avatars for engaging some of the more important contrapuntal images in the poem. Duessa's beast has already been mentioned in connection with avatars as one of several manifestations of the evil principle in serpent form. The series of evil serpents, however, is opposed by a series of serpents associated with virtue. A dragon appears in Arthur's crest, imaging, minimally, the redoubtability of militant virtue.[2]

> His haughtie helmet, horrid all with gold,
> Both glorious brightnesse, and great terrour bred;
> For all the crest a Dragon did enfold
> With greedie pawes, and ouer all did spred
> His golden wings: his dreadfull hideous hed
> Close couched on the beuer, seem'd to throw
> From flaming mouth bright sparkles fierie red,
> That suddeine horror to faint harts did show;
> And scaly tayle was stretcht adowne his backe full low.
>
> [i.vii.31]

The association of the serpent with the ability to inspire fear occurs also in the description of Fidelia's cup, "In which a Serpent did himselfe enfold, / That horrour made to all, that did behold" (i.x.13). The two intertwined serpents of Cambina's rod of peace are compared with those of "the rod which *Maias* sonne doth wield, / Wherewith the hellish fiends he doth confound" (iv.iii.42). The caduceus is a symbol not only of concord but also of the terror by which civil concord may be imposed on the rebellious. In Britomart's dream in the Temple of Isis, the crocodile by his "peerelesse powre" swallows up the storm and flames that threaten the temple (v.vii.14–15). Isis's suppression of the crocodile is the restraint of "those sterne behests, and cruell doomes of his" (v.vii.22), which are allowed scope only when the kingdom is threatened by rebellion. In the context of Book V, the terror of virtue becomes that of executive justice. The vicious counterpart of the crocodile suppressed by Isis (and of its offspring, the lion under Mercilla's feet— cf. v.vii.16 and v.ix.33) is the dragon under the feet of

Lucifera, who "Ne ruld her Realme with lawes, but pollicie" (I.iv.12).[3]

The conjunction of the serpent image with that of the enchanted cup links Duessa with Fidelia as an antitype (Frye, p. 119). It also links her with Fidelia's avatar, Cambina, whose cup contains nepenthe,

> a drinck of souerayne grace,
> Deuized by the Gods, for to asswage
> Harts grief, and bitter gall away to chace,
> Which stirs vp anguish and contentious rage:
> In stead thereof sweet peace and quiet age
> It doth establish in the troubled mynd.   [IV.iii.43]

Those who drink "eternall happinesse do fynd." Both Fidelia's and Cambina's cups calm the passions with the assurance of eternal happiness. As their serpents inspire fear, the contents of their cups quiet the perturbations of the mind with peace. The opposite of their healing effect is the enfeebling property of Duessa's cup and the cups associated with the Bower of Bliss in Book II. Acrasia's enchanted cup (II.i.55), False Genius's "mighty Mazer bowle of wine" (II.xii.49), and the cup of Excesse (II.xii.56) subvert the irascible passions as they serve the will to virtue, whereas the cups of Fidelia and Cambina as agencies of salvation and of friendship assuage the irascible passions of fear and of sorrow and anger, arising from the alienation of the mind from God and from man, that prevent inner calm. Acrasia's cup, like Fidelia's, gives a sense of well being—it too contains wine, "*Bacchus*," and water, "*the Nymph*" (Frye, p. 120)—but its dregs are a gloomy glade.

Associated with virtuous and vicious cups are virtuous and vicious enchantresses, the figures of the priestess and of Circe-Venus that recur in opposition in the poem. Fidelia and Cambina are opposed by such figures as Duessa, Phaedria, Excesse, and Acrasia, who allure their victims by means of a sensuous setting to a dismal end. The earthly

paradise is part of the bait of evil in this form. It appears in
its merest essentials in the setting of Red Cross's dalliance
with Duessa by the enchanted fountain. It appears in the
Garden of Proserpina (II.vii), which, as an antitype of Eden,
offers apples rather than wine, and in the Bower of Bliss,
opposed, in respect to erotic fulfillment and fruition, to the
Garden of Adonis and, in respect to spiritual union, to the
Temple of Venus. The good and evil gardens that appear
here and there in Fairyland are inhabited by good and evil
Venus, Adonis, and Cupid figures. The Bower of Bliss is the
bed chamber of illicit eroticism, just as the Garden of
Adonis is, among other things, that of licit lovemaking.[4]
The victims of Acrasia—Mordant, Cymochles (who is also a
confederate of Acrasia), and Verdant—are, like Red Cross,
Adonis figures, captives of vicious Venuses, whose charms,
unlike those of Venus in the ancient myth, lead to their
death or debilitation.[5] The Venus and Adonis scenes in the
tapestries of the Castle Joyeous (III.i.34–38) and the
triumphs of Cupid in those of the House of Busirane
(III.xi.29–46) appear in sinister contrast to the benign
Venus and Cupid and the mutual, unmitigated pleasure of
the Garden of Adonis. These figures from mythology serve
to align varieties of love as moral opposites in the contexts of
the books in which they appear. Behind the impersonations
of Venus, Adonis, and Cupid and the pleasantness of their
habitations are the deceptive arts of the witch, luring her
victims by fair appearance to the dark dungeon or forest
glade of wasted possibilities. False Venus is Circe disguised.

   The collapsing of Orgoglio like a bladder of air is associated by Joseph Dallett with the sudden disappearances
of Archimago (II.iii.19), Busirane's House (III.xii.43), and
the Snowy Florimell (V.iii.24–25), in opposition to such
disappearances as those of Guyon's guardian angel
(II.viii.8), the dance of the Graces (VI.x.18), and Nature on
Arlo Hill (*Cantos of Mutabilitie,* vii.59). "The first disappear
with the entrance of reason and spiritual rectitude; the

disappearance of the second suggests that certain great
verities lie hidden to mortal view" (p. 111). The phenomenon is an illustration of the similar willingness of vice and
virtue to hide their secrets, the former as a cause and the
latter as a consequence of human wickedness. The revealing
of the true natures of vice and virtue involves the disappearance on the one hand of pretense and on the other of essence
when mortal eyes have beheld as much as they can bear.[6]

Arthur's forced entrance into Orgoglio's Castle, together
with the sumptuous furnishings, the oppressive silence, and
the sense of desolation, links Orgoglio's Castle with the
House of Busirane (III.xi.53) as a great tomb. The discrepancy between the richness above and the filth below recalls
the House of Pride and anticipates the Cave of Mammon
(which are themselves additionally linked by the presence
chambers of Lucifera and Philotime as houses of fame) and
Geryoneo's Temple (V.xi.21, 31–33). The dungeon has
appeared in the House of Pride and will reappear in the
Castle of Corflambo (IV.viii) and in Radigund's iron prison,
where, however, there is companionship in shame and
enough light to enable the prisoners to perform their ignominious tasks (V.v). The altar of idolatrous worship appears in the House of Busirane (III.xi.47) and in Geryoneo's
Temple (V.x.28), and the evidence of human sacrifice in the
House of Pride (I.v.45–53) and in Geryoneo's Temple
(V.xi.19–20). In a sense Lucifera, Philotime, Malecasta,
and Radigund all invite or require false worship, and all the
evil houses are in effect prepared for the destruction of
human victims.[7] These waste houses, in Lewis's phrase, are
vicious resting places that oppose the castles of spiritual
health.[8] Coelia's House of Holiness, Alma's Castle of Temperance, and Mercilla's Palace of Justice serve the questing
knights as places of recuperation and instruction. Each, in
contrast to the castles dominated by vicious women, is under the supervision of a chaste virgin and presents an allegorical anatomy of the virtue she represents. There are

specific oppositions between virtuous and vicious castles. An elaborate antithetical parallelism exists between the House of Pride and the House of Holiness.[9] The ostentation, ease of entrance, surliness and flippancy of the attendants, arrogation of heavenly descent, youth and haughtiness of the ruler, unconcern for petitioners, seven assistants, and view of the lower regions all have their contrasting counterparts in the House of Holiness. The House of Pride is specifically associated with the Palace of Mercilla as an antitype of justice. Both are stately palaces "Of pompous show" (V.ix.21). Both rulers appear in brilliantly decorated presence chambers with glistering thrones. Lucifera, however, is a usurper who rules by policy rather than law. She overawes her petitioners by haughty demeanor rather than by majesty tempered with affability. The dragon beneath her feet is an emblem of the vicious application of force rather than of the force of law, represented by the lion below Mercilla. The artificial glistering of her presence contrasts in quality with the celestial radiance of Mercilla's cloth of state. Other specific oppositions of castles exist in the poem, such as that of the Temple of Venus and the House of Busirane discussed above, but it is the general arrangement of castles in opposing ranks that contributes most significantly to the coherence of the larger parts. As fortresses, storehouses, traps, hospitals, and nurseries, they of all avatars reflect the most comprehensive and, paradoxically, also the most detailed conception of moral struggle in its phases of attack, defense, and recovery. Castles represent enormous concentrations of the energy and intelligence that the reader learns to associate with good and evil in their continuing struggle to expand their frontiers in the human mind.

The stripping of Duessa recalls the exposure of Archimago by, ironically, Sans Loy (I.iii.33–39) and anticipates his exposure by Una (I.xii.33–34) and the baffling of Braggadocchio in Book V (iii.37–39). As avatars of the action of exposure they are closely associated with avatars of disappearance, which image the consequences of exposure. They are opposites of the epiphanies of virtue that occur in the sudden disclosure of the previously concealed beauty of Una (I.xii.21–23); of Belphoebe (II.iii.21–31);[10] of Britomart in the Castle Joyeous (III.i.63), outside Malbecco's Castle (III.ix.20–24), and during her fight with Artegall (IV.vi.19–22). The discoveries of the ugliness and beauty of vicious and virtuous places are also avatars of the uncasing of character. Indeed the concealed ugliness of Duessa is verbally associated with that of the House of Pride, of which "all the hinder parts, that few could spie, / Were ruinous and old, but painted cunningly" (I.iv.5). The dance of the Graces bursts into view with the sudden radiance of epiphany.

The counterpointing of avatars of the revelation of concealed character and of the disappearance of appearance is particularly involved in Spenser's moral purpose to unveil the beauty of virtue and to unmask the ugliness of vice. In the unmasking of vice these avatars are part of the career of the counterfeit, whose destiny in the poem is exposure and exorcism. The counterfeit, as an avatar of concealed evil character, participates with the obvious opposites in the contrapuntal arrangement of similar embodiments of virtue and vice, but it differs from the other opposites in its parading as a good. It is necessary before inquiring further into the contribution of the counterfeit to insist once again on the importance of restricting the distinction of counterfeit and opposite to a perceptual relationship. We must distinguish between expository and fictional identification of fraud.

Conceptual and perceptual counterfeits do not always coincide in the poem. For example, since the Egalitarian Giant expounds a specious justice, he might be regarded as a counterfeit of justice—which indeed he is in terms of the relation of the concept he represents to that represented by

Artegall—but his giant's form does not permit him (despite his scales and fair rhetoric) to masquerade as a good on the fictional level. A counterfeit of justice must, like Dolon, have a hypocritical embodiment. The discrepancy between Dolon's show of hospitality and his malicious intent (v.vi.19–22) is in keeping with the hypocrisy of what he represents as *dolus malus*, "unlawful fraud"—in legal jargon the shrewd manipulation of law for vicious purposes (Lerch, p. 97; Aptekar, p. 116). He is counterfeit justice in embodiment as well as idea.

As a rule, counterfeit virtue is given a counterfeit form. Vicious qualities commonly mistaken as goods masquerade in hypocritical guises. Counterfeit holiness appears in a magician, Archimago; religion in a witch, Duessa; worship in the religious exercises of Corceca; fame in the presence chambers of Lucifera and Philotime; wisdom in the casuistry of Despair; wealth in the treasure house of Mammon; pleasure in the Bower of Bliss; love in the Castle Joyeous; beauty in the Snowy Florimell; justice in Dolon; and courtesy in Mirabella's treatment of her suitors. As conceptual counterfeits, all image spurious goods that are mistakenly regarded as sources of happiness; and as perceptual counterfeits, all are traps through which the unwary may lose the true goods they impersonate.

While contributing didactically in the definition of virtue and the exorcism, by exposure, of vice, the counterfeit supports the coherence of the poem. First, it provides for the intensification of anticipation, recognition, and recollection through dramatic irony. The counterfeit is not qualitatively different from the opposite but rather is a species of opposite in which the revelation of the vicious identity is delayed for the fictional characters. The delayed unmasking provides for a contrast between the knowledge of the reader and the ignorance of the characters who are the targets of deception. The reader is supposed to penetrate the hypocrisy (though generations of romantic critics have been bewitched to the point of thinking Spenser bewitched by Acrasia and her Bower of Bliss). The insistency of the invitation, the garish display of attractions, the conspicuously stereotyped image of virtue with odd discrepancies—all or some of these features conspire, or should conspire, to arouse the uneasiness and suspicion of the reader, if indeed he has not been warned explicitly in the expository passages. (If the reader is deceived, the irony works against him as well as against the character practiced upon by the counterfeiting vice.) The reader's awareness of the vicious identity and purpose of Duessa—implicit in her description (I.ii.13) and companionship with Sans Foy but also explicit in the story of Fradubio (I.ii.32−44) and her confederation with Sans Joy in the House of Pride (I.iv−v), as well as through expository interpolation elsewhere (e.g., I.vii.1−2)—in contrast with the ignorance of Red Cross causes the reader to experience the earlier episodes in relation to likely consequences and to note the progression toward these consequences. The overthrow of Red Cross by Orgoglio, with the connivance of Duessa, is at once the frustration of the expectation of Red Cross and the confirmation of the reader's. The impact upon the reader of the recognition by Red Cross of his error (it is a tacit recognition) is intensified by his previous anticipation. It registers more strongly upon the reader's mind in that it is a consequence that the reader has foreseen.

The heightening of anticipation by the irony not only intensifies recognition but also enhances retrospection at the moment of the unmasking of vice. The awareness of consequence becomes an awareness of and reflection upon antecedents in relation to consequence. The reader is enabled and encouraged, as a result of his previous heightened awareness of the pattern of incidents in relation to their potentialities, to reflect upon the exposure of Duessa in the light of her former actions. The irony intensifies in the reader the response Spenser's characters manifest on witnessing the unmasking of the Snowy Florimell and Braggadocchio:

Now when these counterfeits were thus vncased
Out of the foreside of their forgerie,
And in the sight of all men cleane disgraced,
All gane to iest and gibe full merilie
At the remembrance of their knauerie.
Ladies can laugh at Ladies, Knights at Knights,
To thinke with how great vaunt of brauerie
He them abused, through his subtill slights,
And what a glorious shew he made in all their sights.

[v.iii.39]

This enhancement of anticipation, recognition, and recollection reinforces the concatenation of incidents in the reader's mind, pointing up their causal relations in the narrative.

Second, the image of the counterfeit, with attractive "foreside" and revolting "hinder parts," prophesies or recapitulates (depending on the positioning in the narrative of the full account of its nature) the process of deception undergone by its victims. The tail of Errour is the prototype of the "hinder parts" of the House of Pride and the "neather parts" of Duessa.[11] The discrepancy between fair appearance and foul substance in the description of the counterfeit states visually the contrast between the allurements attending the entrance into temptation and the desolation of "the yssues thereof," which, we are to understand, are "the wayes of death" (Prov. 14:12). The effect is to concretize a segment of narrative into a single image. The language suggests this compression of narrative in the picture of Red Cross, caught quite literally in the consequence of Errour: "God helpe the man so wrapt in *Errours* endlesse traine" (I.i.18).

The counterfeit provides a rich variation within the pattern of anticipation and recollection contributed by avatars and antitypes. There is not only the light of the good and the darkness of the overtly evil, but also the will-o'-the-wisp of false good, flickering here and there, mocking the inexperienced or froward wayfarer in his quest for the true or for another good than the true. The action of counterfeits evokes the labyrinthine convolutions of human experience in a fallen world, in which deception becomes expected. The pattern is familiar enough to readers of modern literature. In Spenser, however, the expectation of deception is a consequence not of disillusioned idealism but rather of an awareness of the resources of evil in its war upon good. Though the counterfeit alone would satisfy the sensibility of modern pessimism and fair appearance alone, without foul consequence, that of naive libertinism and materialism, the entire system of antitypes, including the duplicity of the counterfeit, is necessary to a Christian, as well as to a Ciceronian, conception of a responsible mimesis. Whatever one's moral or mimetic critical criteria, the effect, aesthetically, is a notable reinforcement of the coherence of the poem.

10 · *Architectonic and Organic Unity*

It was impossible to discuss the unifying principles of Parts I and II without reference to multiple embodiments. It was necessary to broach tacitly the subject of avatars in the discussion of the patron knights as partial representations of the concept wholly embodied in Arthur. The discussion of private and public virtue required the consideration of Belphoebe and Gloriana as avatars of the moral character of Elizabeth. In the instances of the impaired quest and of the sloth of the Witch's Son we encountered antitypes of Arthur's magnificence.

In participating in the unifying principles discussed earlier, avatars contribute to the architectonic unity of *The Faerie Queene*. They help to define the formal divisions of the poem and point up the movement from private to public virtue. The unity of the single books is supported by such avatars as the image of the female ruler whose rule is challenged or overthrown (in Belge, Irena, and Mercilla, and in their opposites, Radigund and Duessa) in Book V,[1] and in the doglike behavior of the adversaries of courtesy (e.g., of Defetto, v. 19–20; Turpine, vi. 26; and the Blatant Beast) in Book VI.

Avatars reinforce the association of the books as pairs. Books I and II are drawn together by the reappearance of such images as the dead or dying victim, prostrated before the agent of his destruction (e.g., Despair kneeling beside Terwin, I.ix.36, and Acrasia bending over Verdant, II.xii.76) and the throne rooms of Lucifera (I.iv.6–10) and Philotime (II.vii.43–49), goddesses of false fame. The Cave of Mammon (II.vii) fuses elements of Errour's Den (I.i), the House of Pride (I.iv), Orgoglio's dungeon (I.viii), and the cave of Despair (I.ix): the beaten path, the gloomy half-light, the goddess of false fame, the dark descent to hell, and the aged, cunning rhetorician. Books III and IV are linked by avatars of perverse love. In Book III Timias fights with the Foster, who wounds him with his boar spear (v. 20); in Book IV, with the boarlike Lust (vii. 5, 24–29). Corflambo's pursuit of Placidas (IV.viii) recalls Ollyphant's of the nameless youth (III.xi), and Britomart's pursuit of Ollyphant (III.xi) recalls Palladine's of Argante (III.vii). In the latter two instances, Satyrane is an ineffectual deliverer. In all three a youth is rescued from an equestrian giant whose victims are confined for the sake of perverse desire. Books V and VI are related by such images as the invincible page, the rescue of a lady mistreated by a knight (v.i; VI.i) or other shameless assailant (VI.viii), and the female rebel.[2] We have noticed the importance to the pairing of Books V and VI of Artegall's, Calidore's, and Arthur's roles as avatars of Hercules.

The distinction between the virtues of the odd- and the even-numbered books is supported by avatars. The odd-numbered books reveal the splendor of their virtues by theophany; the even-numbered, by apotheosis. The image of the royal virgin—of Una, Britomart, and Mercilla—appears only in the odd-numbered books, whose patron knights are associated with the history of England. (Britomart does appear in Book IV but not in a context of political significance.) Instances of mediation, both genuine and false, recur in the even-numbered books (compare the peacemaking of Medina, II.ii, and Phaedria, II.vi; of Cambina, IV.iii, and the Squire of Dames, IV.ii; of Calidore, VI.i,iii, and Blandina, VI.iii) in keeping with the concern of these books with earthly harmony (see chap. 6, n. 12).

Avatars help to define the three-book divisions of the poem. The allegorical cores of Books I and II are houses; of

Books IV and V, temples; and of Books III and VI, pleasances.[3] This dichotomy is also reinforced by the giant
image. Pedestrian giants, whose height and terrestrial
affinity are indicated in their lineage as sons of earth and air,
appear in Books I and VI. Equestrian giants, whose
mounted pursuit and flight signify, in terms of the steed
symbolism, the uncontrol and consequent perversion of the
passions, appear in Books III and IV. In Book II a giant
appears in a cave (vii.40–41); in Book V, on a rocky height.
Thus a bilateral symmetry appears within the six books in
terms of this single image. Avatars of character and situation supporting the thematic opposition of duty and felicity
associate the later cantos of Books I and VI and strengthen
the impression of Books I through VI as a rounded unit.
Red Cross's absence from his mission, instruction by aged
wisdom retired from worldly pursuits, ephemeral vision of
felicity, resumption of the quest, and interrupted joy of love
have their counterparts in Calidore's experience in the pas-
toral world of Book VI.

The movement from private to public virtue is supported
by avatars. Of the pleasances that form the allegorical cores
of Books III and VI, the condition of the first is said to be
invulnerable (III.vi.31), as that of the second is revealed to
be vulnerable, to careless or vicious intrusion. The Garden
of Adonis is an inviolable sanctuary, whereas the vision of
the Graces and the idyllic life of the shepherds may be
disrupted by thoughtless curiosity or malicious assault.
With Book VI we have moved into a realm where virtue
may be threatened by external agencies. The movement
from private to public virtue is pointed up by the increasing
incidence of images of wrestling: of Guyon and Furor (II.iv),
Arthur and Maleger (II.xi), Satyrane and the Witch's Beast
(III.vii), Calepine and the bear (VI.iv), Timias and Disdain
(VI.vii), Calidore and Coridon (VI.ix), and Calidore and the
Blatant Beast (VI.xii.30–34). These images, associated
with invulnerability to the sword and with binding and

leading, suggest the necessity of gradualism and containment instead of summary execution and extirpation. They are appropriate to the nature of temperance in Book II and to the attempts of natural virtue to control lust in Book III, but they are especially reflective of the operation of courtesy in its war upon evils entrenched in society. Vice may not be successfully assailed with such rigor in society as in the soul.

A public gathering—or "folke-mote" (IV.iv.6)—is more and more the setting of crucial encounters, or the consequence of such, in the latter books. Simultaneously avatars of slander increase in both frequency and formidability. Whereas the image of the reviling hag appears in Corceca and Abessa (I.iii) and Occasion (II.v) in the first three books, it appears in Sclaunder (IV.viii), Ate (V.ix.47), Envy and Detraction (V.xii), and, though otherwise attractively featured, Briana (VI.i) in the last three.[4] By Book VI slander has become the principal threat to the knight of virtue.

Although avatars contribute importantly to the coherence of the poem by reinforcing the formal structuring, their distinctive value is in providing a coherence that supplements the stricter unity of the scheme of the virtues. It is organic, rather than schematic, unity that is the special contribution of avatars and antitypes. The nature of this contribution has already been examined in regard to the network of avatars and the system of antitypes. It may also be understood and appreciated in relation to the general symbolic terms of the poem.

The basic symbolic oppositions of *The Faerie Queene* are the traditional attributes of virtue and vice. The contrasting qualities of light and dark, height and depth, and order and disorder characterize virtue and vice in both Christian and Platonic thought. In Spenser's allegory they provide a frame of reference for the moral identification of the images and, in so doing, align the images and correlate their meanings according to the fundamental opposition in the poem: the conflict of virtue and vice. The light symbolism participates in the avatars of the epiphany of virtue (e.g., in Red Cross's vision of the New Jerusalem, I.x.58; the unveiling of Una, I.iii.4—7, vi.4, xii.21—23; and the revelation of Britomart's character, III.ix.20) in which the beauty of virtue is represented as a dazzling radiance. Shade is an indicator of religious ignorance or moral turpitude. The Den of Errour is hidden in the shade of a wood (I.i.7). Red Cross twice seeks refuge from the sun in the shade of trees (I.ii.28, vii.3—4), as a consequence and an occasion of the company of Duessa.[5]

Whereas evil as the absence of good is suggested by shade, evil as perverse energy and intelligence is suggested by flaming lamps or beacons—lights within darkness. The "blazing eyes" of the Dragon challenged by Red Cross

> like two bright shining shields,
> Did burne with wrath, and sparkled liuing fyre;
> As two broad Beacons, set in open fields,
> Send forth their flames farre off to euery shyre,
> And warning giue, that enemies conspyre,
> With fire and sword the region to inuade;
> So flam'd his eyne with rage and rancorous yre:
> But farre within, as in a hollow glade,
> Those glaring lampes were set, that made a dreadfull shade.
>
> [I.xi.14]

The Snowy Florimell is given "In stead of eyes two burning lampes" (III.viii.7). From the eyes of Corflambo come "two fierie beames, / More sharpe then points of needles" (IV.viii.39). The "fiery eies" of Disdain "Like two great Beacons, glared bright and wyde" (VI.vii.42). The artificial light of the demonic contrasts with the light of day, emblematic of goodness.

The symbolic opposition of light and dark combines with that of height and depth to identify the cave image with evil. In its possession in combination and to the extremest degree of the two vicious attributes of darkness and depth, the cave is an appropriate dwelling place of the most insidious forms of evil: of Errour, Despair, Mammon, the Witch's Beast, Care, Malengin, Geryoneo's Monster, and the Brigands (Dallett, p. 114). It commonly descends to hell (II.vii.51–63; V.ix.6; VI.x.43, xi.3). Its symbolic opposite is the hill. The Mount of Contemplation, Mount of Venus, and Mount Acidale afford a view of the divine will concerning human life. There are, with two exceptions, no virtuous caves or vicious hills, and the exceptions prove the consistency of the vertical symbolism. Merlin, it is true, dwells in a cave; but his underground abode is, like the "strong rocky Caue" under the Mount of Venus (III.vi.48), a place for the confinement and mastery of potentially destructive forces (III.iii.8–14). The Egalitarian Giant stands upon a rocky eminence (V.ii.30), but he is a figure of extreme presumption; and Talus roughly "shouldered him from off the higher ground, / And down the rock him throwing, in the sea him dround" (V.ii.49).

The symbolic opposition of height and depth combines with both that of light and dark and that of order and disorder (in the humanistic variation of the cultivated and the uncultivated) to identify the "lowly" hermitage of Archimago, "Downe in a dale" and "hard by a forests side" (I.i.34), as an antitype of the hermitage of Contemplation, situated on "an hill, that was both steepe and hy" (I.x.46), and of the cottage of the Hermit of Book VI, which is approached by "a plaine" (v.34). Florimell comes upon the Witch's cottage in "a gloomy hollow glen" in "A little valley . . . / All couerd with thick woods, that quite it ouercame" (III.vii.4–6). Meliboe's cottage, in contrast to the cottages of Archimago and the Witch, as well as of Corceca (I.iii.10) and Sclaunder (IV.viii.23), is situated in "the open fields" (VI.ix.4,16). The three basic symbolic oppositions are thus instrumental in the moral identification of cottages, which, in the historical allegory, represent the establishment of virtue or vice on the common—as the castle, on an institutional—level of society.

The set of symbolic oppositions is important in safeguarding the avatars from misinterpretation and in qualifying their meanings. Belphoebe's pavilion, though deep in a forest, is on "a spatious plaine" (III.v.39). As a huntress whose pursuit of the bestial carries her into the natural domain of vicious impulses, she appropriately dwells in the forest. But her native element, that of virtue, is the light. In contrast Malecasta's House, though approached by "a spatious plaine," is "plaste for pleasure nigh that forrest syde" (III.i.20). Its deceitful character as a Castle Joyeous requires its situation on the plain, but its native element is the darkness and disorder of the forest. Though the uncultivated nature of the Salvage Man is indicated in the location of his dwelling "Farre in a forest," his affinity for virtue is revealed in his preferring to live "by a hollow glade" (cf. the "hollow glen" of the Witch, III.iv.6) as well as in the avoidance of his habitation by the "wyld beasts" (VI.iv.13). Though sustained amidst darkness and disorder, his quality of life is, like Belphoebe's, identified by their antitheses. The dynamic fecundity of the Garden of Adonis and the protective darkness of the pleasant arbor are shielded from the carnal implications of the wildness and gloom of the forest by the orderly arrangement of the seed beds and the height of the Mount of Venus (III.vi.35, 43).

What we have been concerned with in Part III is something more deliberately worked out and controlled than archetypes or mythological structures. Behind the image is a conception generally capable of formulation as an ethical proposition. The image sequence is so ordered as to provide for a developing apprehension of the conception it cumulatively represents. Furthermore it is apparent from the consistency of Spenser's system, or systems, of avatars that the perceptual follows logically and chronologically (in the order of composition) the conceptual. We must therefore take issue with the common notion that "Spenser . . . is a

poet of very limited conceptual powers and is helpless
without some kind of visualization to start him thinking"
(Frye, pp. 111–12). We perceive instead a method and
motive akin to those attributed by Greville to the fiction of
his friend Sidney: "In all these creatures of his making, his
intent, and scope was, to turn the barren Philosophy precepts into pregnant images of life." [6] Ironically the extent to
which he succeeded is the extent to which his poetry may be
appreciated for the mere sake of the images themselves. [7]

CONCLUSION

Critical Justice
and the Giant's Faction

The price of understanding the unity of *The Faerie Queene* is to take seriously the moral allegory. The main unifying principles have a didactic, as well as an aesthetic, rationale, and to disregard the didactic function of the poem is to miss the features that provide its essential coherence. The main obstacle for modern romantic sensibility is not rational but emotional: the obduracy of its religious, moral, and social persuasions. The obstacle looms up formidably in the maddening obstinacy of Shelley's response to Thomas Love Peacock's correction of his interpretation of the episode of the Egalitarian Giant (v.ii). Peacock remarks, "Shelley once pointed out this passage to me, observing, 'Artegall argues with the Giant; the Giant has the best of the argument; Artegall's iron man knocks him over into the sea and drowns him. This is the usual way in which power deals with opinion.' I said, 'That was not the lesson which Spenser intended to convey.' 'Perhaps not,' he said; 'it is the lesson which he conveys to me. I am of the Giant's faction.'" [1]

The poetry of every age has its lessons, and the lessons of Spenser's poetry are not those of Shelley's or those of the poets of today. The problem is compounded for the modern reader in that it is difficult for him, as it was not for Shelley, to conceive of the validity in any age of a view of the world and of human experience very much different from his own. Arnold Stein lays down as his "minimal point" the proposition that "no artist can convince us artistically unless he can make us willing to accept the possible existence of the attitudes he presents." [2] The unwillingness of many a modern reader to entertain the possibility of intelligent belief in ideal virtue requires his interpreting a work like *The Faerie Queene,* if sympathetically, as either an account of the process of disillusionment—of "maturing"—or as an ironic criticism of received ideas. Such a reader's final defense, an expression of both modern obduracy and romantic subjectivism, when confronted with literary and historical evidence is, like Shelley's, "It means what it means to me." Having dismissed the significance of its traditional didacticism, he is left with only the gallery of pictures of the nineteenth-century romantic critics or the fictional and symbolic coherence of modern criticism, and the poem sprawls.[3]

Another obstacle for the reader nourished on the New Criticism is the assumption that only those features may be regarded as relevant to criticism that constitute the differentia between artistic excellence and mediocrity or failure. It is true, as Tuve remarks, that "Spenser in the *Faerie Queene,* insofar as it is a work examining the virtues, wrote something comparable to many lesser preceding pieces" (*Allegorical Imagery,* p. 126). The structures with which we have been concerned are, in their traditional derivation and conventional character, of the kind that requires no unusual genius to devise. Consequently they tend to be dismissed as irrelevant to interpretation and criticism. When the structures of a work happen to be fairly obvious, the work is likely to suffer at the hands of modern critics by either depreciation or misinterpretation. However, one may contend that it is the execution, rather than the implicitness, of the unifying principles of a work that determines its artistic success or failure. One need not scorn the obvious to elicit a proper appreciation for the subtlety of its manifestations.

The intention of this study has not been to minimize the significance of other unifying principles in Spenser's complex creation, but rather to show that the structures deriving from the moral allegory—those explicit in the Letter to

Raleigh and apparent in the poem—are both a necessary and a sufficient cause of its unity. There is of course a twofold risk in essaying a critical excursion in the obvious. One must on the one hand shun the ingenious and on the other somehow circumvent the dull. The reconsideration of the obvious sources and the avoidance of the out-of-the-way, the reiteration of some commonplaces of Spenser criticism, the acceptance at face value of Spenser's statement of intention, and, especially, the subjection of the poem to macroscopic scrutiny may perhaps have enabled us to skirt the Gulfe of Greediness, but it is not at all certain that we have not already split on the Rocke of vile Reproach. Nevertheless, tedious travel is often the most necessary, and if the formal integrity of *The Faerie Queene* is more evident now than before, the enhancement of our appreciation for Spenser's achievement will have justified our endurance of the voyage.

NOTES

Introduction · *The Letter and the Poem*

1. *Edmund Spenser: An Essay on Renaissance Poetry* (London: Edward Arnold, 1925), pp. 50–55. This passage, as well as the passages cited from the writers above, appears in appendix 1 to *The Works of Edmund Spenser: A Variorum Edition,* ed. Edwin Greenlaw et al. (Baltimore: Johns Hopkins Press, 1932–1957), 1:314–62. All citations of Spenser's poetry and prose will refer to this edition.

2. Owen, "The Structure of 'The Faerie Queene,'" *PMLA* 68 (1953): 1079–1100; Bennett, *The Evolution of "The Faerie Queene"* (1942; rpt., New York: Burt Franklin, 1960), pp. 28–29.

3. Spens, *Spenser's Faerie Queene: An Interpretation* (London: Edward Arnold, 1934), chap. 1. Walter, "*The Faerie Queene:* Alterations and Structure," *Modern Language Review* 36 (1941):37–58; "Further Notes on the Alterations to *The Faerie Queene,*" *Modern Language Review* 38 (1943):1–10.

4. *The Poetical Works of Edmund Spenser,* ed. J. C. Smith and Ernest de Selincourt (London: Oxford Univ. Press, 1912), p. li. Cf. Coleridge: "The reader should be carried forward, not merely or chiefly by the mechanical impulse of curiosity, or by a restless desire to arrive at the final solution; but by the pleasurable activity of mind excited by the attractions of the journey itself." *Biographia literaria,* xiv.

5. Lowell: "The true use of him is as a gallery of pictures which we visit as the mood takes us, and where we spend an hour or two at a time, long enough to sweeten our perceptions, not so long as to cloy them." *Spenser's Critics,* ed. William R. Mueller (New York: Syracuse Univ. Press, 1959), p. 93. Lowell's essay was originally published in *North American Review* 120 (April 1875):334–94. The analogy appears in Douglas Bush, *Mythology and the Renaissance Tradition in English Poetry* (Minneapolis: Univ. of Minnesota, 1932), p. 86. The tapestry analogy appears in Graham Hough, *A Preface to The Faerie Queene* (New York: Norton, 1963), p. 94, and in Millar MacLure, "Nature and Art in *The Faerie Queene,*" *ELH* 28 (1961):1–2. The dream analogy appears in Hough, p. 95; Thomas P. Roche, Jr., *The Kindly Flame* (Princeton Univ. Press, 1964), pp. 32–34; Arnold Williams,

Flower on a Lowly Stalk (E. Lansing: Michigan State Univ. Press, 1967), pp. 124–27. An illustration of the revolution in taste since Spenser's time is the pejorative application of the dream analogy to the coherence of *The Faerie Queene* by William Davenant: "His Allegoricall Story (by many held defective in the Connexion) resembling (me thinks) a continuance of extraordinary Dreams: such as excellent Poets, and Painters, by being over-studious may have in the beginning of Fevers," from *A Discourse upon Gondibert . . .* (1650), in *Spenser: The Critical Heritage,* ed. R. M. Cummings (London: Routledge and Kegan Paul, 1971), p. 187.

6. W.B.C. Watkins and E.M.W. Tillyard suggest that Book VI, like the last plays of Shakespeare, gives a satisfying sense of finality to the author's accomplishment: *Shakespeare and Spenser* (Princeton Univ. Press, 1953), p. 58; *The English Epic and Its Background* (New York: Oxford Univ. Press, 1954), p. 286. The same view is held by Northrop Frye, "The Structure of Imagery in *The Faerie Queene,*" *University of Toronto Quarterly* 30 (1961):110–11; Donald Cheney, *Spenser's Image of Nature* (New Haven: Yale Univ. Press, 1966), p. 239; Kathleen Williams, *Spenser's World of Glass* (Berkeley: Univ. of California Press, 1966), p. xvii; Joanne F. Holland, "The Cantos of Mutabilitie and the Form of *The Faerie Queene,*" *ELH* 35 (1968):21–31; Richard Neuse, "Book VI as Conclusion to *The Faerie Queene,*" *ELH* 35 (1968):329–53; Maurice Evans, *Spenser's Anatomy of Heroism* (Cambridge: Cambridge Univ. Press, 1970), pp. 237–39. Sheldon P. Zitner, in his introduction to *The Mutabilitie Cantos* (London: Nelson, 1968), surveys the views of the relationship of the *Cantos* to Books I through VI and states his own view of the *Cantos* as climaxing the poem. For a view of the poem as "theoretically endless," see Roger Sale, *Reading Spenser: An Introduction to The Faerie Queene* (New York: Random House, 1968), p. 10 (source of the phrase); John Arthos, *On the Poetry of Spenser and the Form of Romances* (London: Allen and Unwin, 1956), pp. 183–84; Cheney, p. 17. Judith Dundas defends the importance of the scheme of the virtues and the validity of the plan described in the Letter while still affirming the unity of the poem as it exists, in "*The Faerie Queene:* The Incomplete Poem and the Whole Meaning," *Modern Philology* 71 (1974):257–65.

7. Fowler, "Numerical Composition in *The Faerie Queene*," *Journal of the Warburg and Courtauld Institute* 25 (1962):199–239; *Spenser and the Numbers of Time* (London: Routledge and Kegan Paul, 1964). Studies of the *Amoretti* and *Epithalamion* have established Spenser's concern with numerological (especially calendrical) structuring: A. Kent Hieatt, *Short Time's Endless Monument* (New York: Columbia Univ. Press, 1960); Alexander Dunlop, "The Unity of Spenser's *Amoretti*," in *Silent Poetry: Essays in Numerological Analysis,* ed. Alastair Fowler (London: Routledge and Kegan Paul, 1970), pp. 153–69; O. B. Hardison, Jr., "*Amoretti* and the *Dolce Stil Nuovo*," *English Literary Renaissance* 2 (1972):208–16.

8. Nelson, *The Poetry of Edmund Spenser* (New York: Columbia Univ. Press, 1963), p. 116; Ellrodt, *Neoplatonism in the Poetry of Spenser* (Geneva: Droz, 1960), p. 59; Fowler, *Numbers of Time,* p. 51.

9. *Allegorical Imagery* (Princeton: Princeton Univ. Press, 1966), p. 358.

10. Donald Baker, while accepting A. C. Hamilton's defense of the Letter as a historiographer's account, as distinct from the poem as the poet's account, still believes Hamilton goes too far in saying that "if the Letter is properly read . . . there are no divergencies with the poem." The two accounts of Guyon's quest cannot be made to agree. "Here clearly, however one may slice it, Spenser slipped." "The Accuracy of Spenser's *Letter to Raleigh*," *Modern Language Notes* 76 (1961):103–4; Hamilton, "Spenser's *Letter to Raleigh*," *Modern Language Notes* 73 (1958):485.

11. "Genre, Milieu, and the 'Epic Romance,'" in *English Institute Essays,* 1951, ed. Alan S. Downer (1952; rpt., New York: AMS, 1965), p. 110.

12. "First Commentary on *The Faerie Queene:* Annotations in Lord Bessborough's Copy of the First Edition of *The Faerie Queene*," *Times Literary Supplement,* 9 April 1964, p. 294. Paul Alpers challenges the representativeness of the annotator, noting the equal responsiveness of the age to sensuous description, in *The Poetry of The Faerie Queene* (Princeton: Princeton Univ. Press, 1967), pp. 152–59. Obviously the two responses were not regarded as mutually exclusive in Spenser's age, as they have been so often since.

13. *Observations on the Fairy Queen of Spenser* (1762; rpt., New York: Haskell House, 1969), 1:9–10.

14. "Is not Spenser's 'larger outline,' the schematic organization of *The Faerie Queene*, the aspect of the poem that is easiest to apprehend and that most takes care of itself as we are reading? Is not Spenser's verse most involving, complex, and illuminating precisely when we are paying attention to its details?" (p. 107).

1 · *The Nurturing of an Exemplar*

1. Nelson, pp. 121–22, objects to construing *fashion* as "educate or train," citing instances to show that *fashion*, in a literary-critical context, meant simply "represent" or "delineate."

2. *An Apologie for Poetry* (London, 1595), in *Elizabethan Critical Essays*, ed. G. Gregory Smith (Oxford: Clarendon, 1904), 1:157.

3. *De inventione*, II.liv, in *De Inventione, De Optima Genere Oratorum, and Topica*, trans. H. M. Hubbell (London: Heinemann, 1949).

4. Ed. W. Nelson Francis, Early English Text Society, vol. 217 (London: Oxford Univ. Press, 1942), pp. 168–69. Cited (in Caxton's translation) by Tuve, to whose discussion of magnificence mine is substantially indebted.

5. *The Works of Geoffrey Chaucer*, ed. F. N. Robinson (Boston: Houghton Mifflin, 1957), p. 251.

6. Chaucer's Parson discusses fortitude and its "speces" as "*Remedium contra peccatum Accidie.*"

7. *Books I and II of The Faerie Queene, The Mutability Cantos, and Selections from the Minor Poetry*, ed. Robert Kellogg and Oliver Steele (New York: Odyssey, 1965), p. 331, note to II.ix.3–7.

2 · *The Garden of Virtue*

1. Artegall, like Red Cross, is a changeling. He was taken to Fairyland "in infant cradle" (III.iii.26), not by Astraea.

2. The use of *mirror* in this sense occurs in I.Pro.4 and II.iii.25.

3. I am reading "faire mirrhour," "lond of Faery," and "antique Image" as equivalents.

4. Isabel E. Rathborne, *The Meaning of Spenser's Fairyland* (New York: Columbia Univ. Press, 1937), pp. 104–28.

5. In 928 Aethelstan banished the West Welsh from Exeter and made the Tamar the boundary of West Wales, so that Wales, in an ancient sense, implied the entire region inhabited by the native British: not only modern Wales but also Cornwall and part of Devonshire. Charles Bowie Millican has remarked that Wales is divided by the river Severn or thereabouts from Fairyland, which is "Elizabethan England." *Spenser and the Table Round,* Harvard Studies in Comparative Literature, no. 8 (1932; rpt., New York: Octagon, 1967), pp. 145–46.

6. *The Expansion of Elizabethan England* (New York: St. Martin's, 1955), chaps. 1 and 2.

7. The geographical symbolism has biblical and classical analogues. Whereas the western boundary of England demarks immature and mature moral character in *The Faerie Queene,* the southern and eastern boundary of Palestine demarks immature and mature spiritual character in New Testament writings. In 2 Corinthians 3 and Hebrews 3, the Land of Promise signifies Christian maturity, and the wilderness of Sinai, setting of the wanderings of Israel before its passage into the Promised Land, represents carnal Christianity. Paul in Galatians 4 associates Mount Sinai with a legalistic adherence to ritual and a reliance upon a righteousness of works, and Jerusalem with the liberty of the Christian under the New Covenant of grace. Whereas Israel had remained in Egypt for four hundred years before returning under Moses to Palestine, the Britons, says Spenser, had been banished from England for "twise foure hundreth yeares" (III.iii.44). On entering Palestine, the Hebrews, like Spenser's Britons and particularly Arthur, encountered fierce antagonists, including giants and tyrants, that had to be subdued before the center of political rule could be established at Jerusalem. The tendency of patristic writers, following Origen, to allegorize the wars of the Hebrews gives additional plausibility to this analogue as a source of Spenser's conception. A Virgilian analogue is the allegorical interpretation of the adventures of Aeneas. From Fulgentius onward, Aeneas's career was understood to represent

moral development from youth to maturity, as well as a progression from contemplative or private virtue to active or political virtue. Aeneas's arrival in Italy signaled the mature exercise of his powers in a series of battles leading, like Arthur's, to the establishment by royal marriage of an imperial dynasty.

8. On the virtues as loves, see Ernst R. Curtius, *European Literature and the Latin Middle Ages,* trans. Willard R. Trask, Bollingen Series, no. 36 (Princeton: Princeton Univ. Press, 1953), p. 523.

9. Trans. F. H. Colson and G. H. Whitaker, II.36–38, in *Philo* (London: Heinemann, 1929), 3:231. All citations of Philo's works refer to this edition.

10. *Allegorical Interpretation of Genesis,* trans. G. H. Whitaker, 1.43–47. Alastair Fowler attributes the name "Guyon" to the association of the rivers of Eden with the cardinal virtues, Gihon with temperance. "Emblems of Temperance in *The Faerie Queene,* Book II," *Review of English Studies* 11 (1960):147; "The River Guyon," *Modern Language Notes* 75 (1960):289–92.

11. *On Husbandry,* trans. F. H. Colson and G. H. Whitaker, 8–10, 17–18.

12. Golding cites it in the preface to his translation of Ovid's *Metamorphoses.* Josephine Bennett points out that at Cambridge Philo was read along with the *Timaeus* for the master's degree. His works were available in translation by John Christopherson (d. 1558), a onetime fellow of Spenser's college, Pembroke Hall. Philo's commentary "was standard," for he was regarded as a Christian. "Spenser's Garden of Adonis Revisited," *Journal of English and Germanic Philology* 41 (1942):60–61.

13. Arnold Williams, *The Common Expositor: An Account of the Commentaries on Genesis, 1527–1633* (Chapel Hill: Univ. of North Carolina Press, 1948), p. 110. See also *The New Schaff-Herzog Religious Encyclopedia,* ed. Samuel Macauley Jackson (New York: Funk and Wagnalls, 1910), 8:348, "Paradise," for a concise account of the views.

14. *Paradise,* trans. John J. Savage, 12–14, in *Fathers of the Church* (New York: Fathers of the Church, 1961), 42:294–96.

15. Marcellus Palingenius, *The Zodiake of Life,* trans. Barnabe Googe (1576; rpt., New York: Scholars' Facsimiles and Reprints, 1947), pp. 172–73. William Shakespeare, *The Complete Plays*

and Poems, ed. William Allan Neilson and Charles Jarvis Hill (Cambridge, Mass.: Houghton Mifflin, 1942), *Othello,* I.iii. 322–29. All citations of Shakespeare's works will refer to this edition.

16. *De Principiis,* trans. Frederick Crombie, II.xi.6, in *The Ante-Nicene Fathers,* ed. Alexander Roberts and James Donaldson, vol. 4 (Buffalo: Christian Literature Publishing Company, 1885), p. 299. See *Cyclopaedia of Biblical, Theological, and Ecclesiastical Literature,* ed. John M'Clintock and James Strong (New York: Harper, 1891), 7:658, "Paradise," for a concise history of the concept.

17. *The Anticlaudian of Alain de Lille,* trans. William Hafner Cornog (Philadelphia: Univ. of Pennsylvania, 1935), VI.iv, IX.viii.

18. The curious reference to Aristotle has been variously accounted for as the result of a haziness of memory (Viola Hulbert, *Variorum,* 1:356) or as an evidence of the stubborn independence of the poet's mind (Renwick, *Variorum,* 1:361). The phrase "as Aristotle hath deuised" has been explained as modifying "perfected," rather than "vertues," and therefore meaning not an identical list but a similar manner of treatment: *Variorum* editors, 1:343; Jerry Leath Mills, "Spenser's Letter to Raleigh and the Averroistic *Poetics," English Language Notes* 14 (1977):246–49. Renwick takes it to mean "such as Aristotle would call *private* virtues" (*Variorum,* 1:361). Spenser's citing of "Aristotle and the rest" in support of his conception of magnificence has suggested to Viola Hulbert that Spenser's indebtedness to Aristotle was only indirect by way of the many interpreters whose commentaries stood between the poet and the original text (*Variorum,* 1:353–57).

19. "Plan of the 'Faerie Queene,'" *Notes and Queries,* 4th ser., 4 (1869):211–12.

20. Tuve, p. 443; *Commentary on the Dream of Scipio,* trans. William Harris Stahl (New York: Columbia Univ. Press, 1952), I.viii.7–8, p. 122; *Bibliotheca Eliotae,* rev. Thomas Cooper (London, 1559).

21. Macrobius continued to exercise a direct, as well as an indirect, influence upon men of learning in the Renaissance. Gabriel Harvey, for example, remarks that he had been reading

Macrobius's *Dialogues of the Saturnalia* the week before returning to Oxford to lecture on Cicero. *Gabriel Harvey's Ciceronianus,* ed. Harold S. Wilson, trans. Clarence A. Forbes, University of Nebraska Studies in the Humanities, no. 4 (Lincoln: Univ. of Nebraska, 1945), pp. 56–57. Also, E. K. refers to and borrows heavily from Book I of the *Saturnalia,* which discusses the calendar, in his account of "the generall argument" of *The Shepheardes Calender.* Nelson, p. 170, finds echoes of Cicero's *Somnium Scipionis* in passages in Book I concerned with Red Cross's despair, both in the Cave of Despair and in the House of Holiness. Ellrodt assumes the source to have been Macrobius's commentary (I.viii), "a medieval textbook still in favor in the XVIth century" (p. 53, n. 31).

22. *A Discourse of Ciuill Life* (London, 1606), p. 214.

23. *Natural History,* trans. H. Rackham and W.H.S. Jones (London: Heinemann, 1950), XVII.xii.

3 · Active Virtue

1. See Robert E. Kaske, *"Sapientia et Fortitudo* as the Controlling Theme of *Beowulf," Studies in Philology* 55 (1958):423–57, reprinted in *An Anthology of Beowulf Criticism,* ed. Lewis E. Nicholson (Notre Dame: Univ. of Notre Dame Press, 1963), pp. 269–310; Curtius, p. 175; and John M. Steadman, *Milton and the Renaissance Hero* (Oxford: Clarendon, 1967), pp. 9–12, for discussions of this concept as an epic formula.

2. In the persons of Elizabeth it blends with the legal and political doctrine of "the king's two bodies." Nelson, pp. 123–25; Ernest H. Kantorowicz, *The King's Two Bodies* (Princeton: Princeton Univ. Press, 1957).

3. Aquinas quotes Gregory (*Moralium libri,* vi) with approval: "the contemplative life has greater merit than the active life," *Summa Theologica,* Fathers of the English Dominican Province (New York: Benziger Brothers, 1947–1948), I–II, q. 57, art. 2; see also I–II, q. 66, art. 4. The superiority of contemplation appears clearly in Dante's *Paradiso* in the hierarchy of the virtues according to the heavenly spheres. The Renaissance view is definitively stated by Cicero: "This, then, may be regarded as

settled: in choosing between conflicting duties, that class takes precedence which is demanded by the interests of human society." *De Officiis*, trans. Walter Miller (London: Heinemann, 1947), I.xlv.160. On the Renaissance ideal of active virtue and the utilitarian character of English Renaissance humanism, see Margaret Greaves, *The Blazon of Honour: A Study in Renaissance Magnanimity* (London: Methuen, 1964), pp. 65–66, and Douglas Bush, *The Renaissance and English Humanism* (Toronto: Univ. of Toronto Press, 1939), pp. 78–79, respectively.

4. Barclay's poem (1570; rpt., Manchester: Spenser Society, 1885) is a translation of Dominicus Mancinus's *De quattor virtutibus*. The passage cited is on p. 27.

5. Guazzo, *La Civile Conversatione,* trans. George Pettie and Bartholomew Young (London, 1586), 1:56, quoted by John Leon Lievsay, *Stefano Guazzo and the English Renaissance* (Chapel Hill: Univ. of North Carolina Press, 1960), p. 36; Lipsius, *Six Bookes of Politickes or Ciuil Doctrine,* trans. William Jones (London, 1594), p. 1; Hurault, *Politicke, Moral, and Martial Discourses,* trans. Arthur Golding (London, 1595), p. 1.

6. "Spenser's Influence on *Paradise Lost*," *Studies in Philology* 17 (1920):359.

7. All biblical quotations refer to the Geneva version, 1560 edition.

8. William O. Harris in *Skelton's Magnyfycence and the Cardinal Virtue Tradition* (Chapel Hill: Univ. of North Carolina Press, 1965), pp. 63–67, discusses Aquinas's association of, and distinction between, *magnificence* and *magnanimity.*

4 · *Complementary Association in Pairs*

1. *The Figure of the Poet in Renaissance Epic* (Cambridge, Mass.: Harvard Univ. Press, 1965), p. 212. Durling does not infer any structural purpose from the distribution of these authorial intrusions.

2. The three-book level was, of course, undefined by the ending of Book III in the 1596 edition, and we do not know how, or even whether, the ending of Book VI might have been altered,

like that of Book III, with the publication of another installment. The three-book level does, however, remain distinct in the positioning of the cardinal virtues in relation to the other virtues and to each other.

3. The extreme of this tendency is exemplified in Paul Alpers's contention that "the basic large unit in *The Faerie Queene* is the canto, not the book," and that, accordingly, Spenser "does not expect our span of attention and retention to last for more than about a canto, or at most two" (p. 107).

4. E.g., Cheney, p. 17; K. Williams, *Spenser's World of Glass*, pp. 87–91; James Carscallen, "The Goodly Frame of Temperance: The Metaphor of Cosmos in *The Faerie Queene*, Book II," *University of Toronto Quarterly* 37 (1968):153. For a background of the idea of *discordia concors* see Edgar Wind, *Pagan Mysteries in the Renaissance* (New Haven: Yale Univ. Press, 1958), pp. 81–88. A concise account appears in Earl Wasserman, *The Subtler Language* (Baltimore: Johns Hopkins Press, 1959), pp. 53–54, and a comprehensive treatment in Leo Spitzer, "Classical and Christian Ideas of World Harmony," *Traditio* 2 (1944):409–64; 3 (1945):307–64. Rosamund Tuve shows its medieval vitality in "A Medieval Commonplace in Spenser's Cosmology," *Studies in Philology* 30 (1933):133–47.

5. Books I and II have been associated by E. A. Strathman, *Variorum,* 2:467; H.S.V. Jones, *A Spenser Handbook* (New York: Crofts, 1930), p. 172; Edwin Greenlaw, *Studies in Spenser's Historical Allegory* (Baltimore: Johns Hopkins Press, 1932), p. 89; Bennett, *Evolution,* pp. 124–37; A.S.P. Woodhouse, "Nature and Grace in *The Faerie Queene*," *ELH* 16 (1949):204–8; Watkins, p. 173 (though with reservations); Virgil Whitaker, "The Theological Structure of the *Faerie Queene*, Book I," *ELH* 19 (1952):151–64; A. C. Hamilton, "Like Race to Runne: The Parallel Structure of *The Faerie Queene*, Books I and II," *PMLA* 73 (1958):327–34; A. B. Giamatti, *The Earthly Paradise and the Renaissance Epic* (Princeton: Princeton Univ. Press, 1966), pp. 247–49. Books III and IV have been associated by John Erskine, *Variorum,* 4:289; C. G. Osgood, "Comments on the Moral Allegory of the *Faerie Queene*," *Modern Language Notes* 46 (1931):503–4; C. S. Lewis, *The Allegory of Love* (1936; rpt., New

York: Oxford Univ. Press, 1958), pp. 338–39, 346–47; Bennett, *Evolution,* pp. 138, 164; W.J.B. Owen, "The Structure of 'The Faerie Queene,'" p. 1091; Maurice Evans, "Platonic Allegory in *The Faerie Queene,*" *Review of English Studies* NS 12 (1961):132; Hamilton, *The Structure of Allegory in The Faerie Queene* (Oxford: Oxford Univ. Press, 1961), pp. 138–69; K. Williams, "Venus and Diana: Some Uses of Myth in *The Faerie Queene,*" *ELH* 28 (1961):101–20; Roche, *Kindly Flame,* pp. 195–211 (esp. p. 202); K. Williams, *Spenser's World of Glass,* pp. 79–80, 122; Evans, *Spenser's Anatomy of Heroism,* pp. 151, 179–80. Books V and VI have been associated by B.E.C. Davis, *Edmund Spenser: A Critical Study* (1933; rpt., New York: Russell and Russell, 1962), though only as having antithetical heroes and milieus; P. C. Bayley, "Order, Grace, and Courtesy in Spenser's World," in *Patterns of Love and Courtesy: Essays in Memory of C. S. Lewis,* ed. John Lawlor (Evanston, Ill.: Northwestern Univ. Press, 1966), pp. 182, 188–89; Cheney, pp. 175–96; Christie Lerch, "Spenser's Ideal of Civil Life: Justice and Charity in Books V and VI of *The Faerie Queene*" (Ph.D. diss., Bryn Mawr, 1966), pp. 1–2 et passim; K. Williams, *Spenser's World of Glass,* pp. 192–95; Arnold Williams, *Flower on a Lowly Stalk,* p. 42 (tacitly); Evans, *Spenser's Anatomy of Heroism,* p. 209. Books I and II and Books III and IV have been regarded as pairs by Tillyard, p. 287; Arthos, p. 196; Hough, p. 235. The arrangement in pairs of all the books is suggested by Roche, p. 200; Cheney, p. 190 (tacitly); Lerch, pp. 225–26; and Evans, *Spenser's Anatomy of Heroism,* p. 209.

6. "But wretched we, where ye haue left your marke, / Must now anew begin, like race to runne" (II.i.32); "But where ye ended haue, now I begin / To tread an endlesse trace" (VI.i.6). In I.ix.1 Spenser explains the accord of the knights of virtue as indicating an affinity between the virtues they represent.

7. A.C. Hamilton in "Like Race to Runne: The Parallel Structure of *The Faerie Queene,* Books I and II" provides a detailed discussion of the parallelism.

8. E.g., J. H. Walter, "'The Faerie Queene': Alterations and Structure," pp. 47–48.

9. Harris, pp. 71–114, shows the importance of pride and

despair as sins associated with prosperity and adversity in the double-conflict pattern of the morality plays and in Skelton's *Magnyfycence.*

10. Jones, "The *Faerie Queene* and the Medieval Aristotelian Tradition," *Journal of English and Germanic Philology* 25 (1926):286; Padelford, "The Virtue of Temperance in the *Faerie Queene,*" *Studies in Philology* 18 (1921):336. Woodhouse strenuously argued against the existence of a synthesis of nature and grace in Book II as a blurring of his distinction of the two orders; in fact he placed Books III–VI, as well as Book II, within the order of nature. See also "Nature and Grace in Spenser: A Rejoinder," *Review of English Studies* NS 6 (1955):284–88, and "Spenser, Nature and Grace: Mr. Gang's Mode of Argument Reviewed," *ELH* 27 (1960):1–15. Woodhouse's view has been challenged by Alastair Fowler, who argues that the milieu of Book II is also theological, that Guyon's career relates to Red Cross's as sanctification to regeneration. "The Image of Mortality: The *Faerie Queene,* II.i–ii," *Huntington Library Quarterly* 24 (1961):91–110. Woodhouse's and Fowler's constructions of the domains of the books are not mutually exclusive. Spenser assigns temperance in particular and pagan ethics in general to the process of sanctification, distinguishing their province from that of justification and regeneration, which are the work of faith. In Pauline and Petrine theology, the office of temperance and the other virtues is posterior to that of faith (Eph. 2:8–10; 2 Pet. 1:5–7). Bush, *The Renaissance and English Humanism.*

11. Spenserian temperance conflates the Aristotelian doctrine of the mean between excess and defect with the Thomistic counterpoising of the irascible and concupiscible passions. Cf. II.i.58 and *Summa Theologica,* I, q. 81, art. 3.

12. Carscallen, pp. 136–55.

13. Owen, "Structure of 'The Faerie Queene,'" p. 1091; Osgood, pp. 503–4 (Lewis, p. 338, is in agreement: "we are justified in treating them as a single book on the subject of love"). On their mythic structure, see Hamilton, *Structure of Allegory in The Faerie Queene,* pp. 138–69; K. Williams, "Venus and Diana," pp. 101–20. Roche, p. 202; see especially the final chapter, "Conclusion: Structure as Meaning," for a succinct account of the structural relationships and thematic continuity.

14. Walter, "Further Notes," p. 9; H. Clement Notcutt, *"The Faerie Queene* and Its Critics," in *Essays and Studies by Members of the English Association* 12 (1926):74–78.

15. To read the episode of the Temple of Venus as a solution to Scudamour's present distress (it being an account of his winning of Amoret) is at once fictionally inconsistent and allegorically proper. It is true that the adventure happened before their separation, but Scudamour's recounting it after the dissipation of his jealousy and of Amoret's fear supports its significance as an ideal of mental courtship. Amoret, in a sense, was not fully won before. It is allegorical rather than narrative logic that is chiefly responsible for the order of incidents in *The Faerie Queene.*

16. Williams, *Spenser's World of Glass,* pp. 192–93, and Cheney, pp. 186–87, 189, see thematic definition in the Munera-Pollente and Briana-Crudor episodes. Cheney regards the invincible pages as a parallel feature (p. 213) and Calepine and Salvage as complementary characters (p. 196).

17. The linking episodes at the end of Book V and the beginning of Book VI have been discussed by Cheney, pp. 178–81; K. Williams, *Spenser's World of Glass,* pp. 193–95; A. Williams, *Flower on a Lowly Stalk,* pp. 42–43; Bayley, pp. 178–88; and Evans, *Spenser's Anatomy of Heroism,* p. 209.

18. Lerch: "The 'quest' for the just society requires the participation of both Artegall and Calidore, and is not complete until Calidore sees the vision of the Graces" (p. 2). Cheney also makes this point: "In a number of ways, then, Book V may be seen as a preparation for Book VI, which it requires for an imaginatively satisfying conclusion" (p. 174).

19. *Dialogue between Reginald Pole and Thomas Lupset* (c. 1530), p. 185, quoted by Lerch, p. 42.

20. "An Exhortation Concerning Good Order and Obedience to Rulers and Magistrates," in *The Two Books of Homilies,* ed. John Griffiths (Oxford: Oxford Univ. Press, 1859), p. 107, quoted by Lerch, p. 38. Lerch's dissertation provides the fullest and most illuminating account of Spenser's concept of civil justice.

21. *The Six Bookes of a Commonweale,* trans. Richard Knolles (London, 1606), vi.i, p. 644.

22. E.g., Bodin: "The periodic reformation of abuses [by the censors] was one of the best and most excellent measures that was

4

206   *Notes*

euer introduced into any commonwealth, and the one which most contributed to the preseruation of the Roman Empire" (p. 182).

23. *De re publica,* IV.vi, in *De Re Publica, De Legibus,* trans. Clinton Walker Keyes (London: Heinemann, 1928).

24. IV.xi, p. 103. The censor is to exercise his office against "Wantonesse, lust, drunkennesse, quarrels, periuries, and all such other things, which Honestie & Modestie do condemne," including "idlenesse" and "excesse" (pp. 103–4). Lipsius goes beyond Cicero in recommending the use of punishment, as well as shame, because of the decay of manners "now adayes": "Surely I would chastize them, and trace them out certaine markes vpon their brazen forehead, where no blood were left" (pp. 105–6).

25. K. Williams, *Spenser's World of Glass,* p. 194; Jean MacIntyre, "Spenser's Herculean Heroes," *Humanities Association of Canada Bulletin* 17 (1966):5–12; Bayley, pp. 188–89. Explicit references to Hercules occur in v.i.2–3, v.24, viii.31; VI.xii.32,35.

26. Dunseath, *Spenser's Allegory of Justice in Book Five of The Faerie Queene* (Princeton: Princeton Univ. Press, 1968), pp. 46–67 et passim; Aptekar, *Icons of Justice* (New York: Columbia Univ. Press, 1969), pp. 153–214. Antecedents of these detailed discussions are Rathborne, pp. 88–104; K. Williams, "Venus and Diana," pp. 104–16; and Nelson, p. 257. Aptekar develops at length Williams's suggestion, p. 116, of the ambiguity of the Hercules tradition and Spenser's exploitation of its potentiality for ambivalent characterization.

27. Dunseath, pp. 73–76, notices this allusion to Hercules' labors.

28. Lerch, p. 31, remarks that "the 'cutting' away of evils in the commonwealth . . . is exactly Artegall's function in Book V" and refers to Spenser's statement in *A Vewe of the Present State of Irelande* that "the cuttinge of all that nacion with the sworde . . . neuer will become good" (*Variorum,* 9:148).

29. Trans. Paul Shorey (London: Heinemann, 1937), IV.425, 427.

30. P. 10. Cf. Calidore's fair speech to Briana (i.26–28); to Tristram (ii.24–26); to Priscilla (ii.45–46; iii.9), Aladine (iii.14), and Priscilla's father (iii.18); to Calepine (iii.22); to Meliboe (ix.18,27–28,31–32); to Colin (x.29); and to Coridon (xi.35).

31. *Complete Poems and Major Prose,* ed. Merritt Y. Hughes (New York: Odyssey, 1957), p. 733.

32. "Law and Manners," *The Atlantic Monthly* 134 (July 1924):1.

33. Ruth Kelso, *The Doctrine of the English Gentleman in the Sixteenth Century* (Urbana: Univ. of Illinois Press, 1929), p. 88.

34. *Marcus Tullius Ciceroes Thre Bookes of Duties* (London, 1558), 1:fol.43–44.

35. P. 13, in *Four Political Treatises, 1533–1541*, ed. Lillian Gottesman (Gainesville, Fla.: Scholars' Facsimiles and Reprints, 1967), p. 219. See also *I Henry IV*, III.ii.50, for the use of *courtesy* in this sense.

36. *The Governour,* ed. Henry Herbert Stephen Croft (1883; rpt., New York: Burt Franklin, 1967), 2:88–89.

37. Lerch, pp. 166–67, regards VI.i.26 as defining the subjects of Books V and VI as justice and humanity, though she prefers the term *charity* to designate the virtue of VI and gives no further attention to humanity as a virtue. Cf. Cheney, p. 182.

38. (London, 1579), pp. 14–15, in "Haly Heron: Elizabethan Essayist and Euphuist," *Huntington Library Quarterly* 16 (1952):14.

39. D. S. Brewer, "Courtesy and the Gawain-Poet," in *Patterns of Love and Courtesy,* pp. 54–85, and Bayley, pp. 197–98, show the connotations *courtesy* had acquired by Spenser's time.

5 · *Cumulative Progression within Pairs*

1. Evans, "The Fall of Guyon," *ELH* 28 (1961):222; Berger, *The Allegorical Temper* (New Haven: Yale Univ. Press, 1957).

2. "Like Race to Runne," p. 334.

3. K. Williams, *Spenser's World of Glass,* pp. 79–80, 122.

4. *De amicitia,* vii.24, in *De Senectute, De Amicitia, De Divinatione,* trans. William Armistead Falconer (London: Heinemann, 1927), p. 135.

5. Roche, p. 224, regards courtship as the domain of Book III.

6. A. Kent Hieatt, "Scudamour's Practice of Maistrye upon Amoret," *PMLA* 77 (1962):510.

7. These episodes have been compared by K. Williams, *Spenser's World of Glass,* pp. 79–80, 105–7; MacLure, pp. 18–19; Hieatt, "Scudamour's Practice of Maistrye," p. 510; Roche, pp. 130–31; and Mark Rose, *Heroic Love: Studies in Sidney and Spenser* (Cambridge, Mass.: Harvard Univ. Press, 1968), pp. 119–21.

8. Roche, pp. 128–30; Hieatt, "Scudamour's Practice of Maistrye," pp. 509–10.

9. Joseph B. Dallett, "Ideas of Sight in *The Faerie Queene,*" *ELH* 27 (1960):114; Bayley, p. 191. It is true that caves appear prominently in Books I, II, and IV; but in Books V and VI they are assailed deliberately as strongholds rather than approached unwittingly or unwisely by intended victims.

10. The following analysis of the structure of Book V is generally indebted to the excellent study by James Phillips, "Renaissance Concepts of Justice and the Structure of *The Faerie Queene,* Book V," *Huntington Library Quarterly* 33 (1970):103–120.

11. Graziani, "Elizabeth at Isis' Church," *PMLA* 79 (1964): 376–89; Kermode, *"The Faerie Queene,* I and V," *Bulletin of the John Rylands Library* 47 (1964):123–50.

12. W. Nicholas Knight in "The Narrative Unity of Book V of *The Faerie Queene:* 'That Part of Justice Which Is Equity,'" *Review of English Studies* NS 21 (1970):287, interprets the trial thus, but his identification of Mercilla as equity is not, I think, precise.

13. I.xxii.3, in *Moral Essays,* trans. John W. Basore (London: Heinemann, 1928), 1:418–21.

14. Knight, p. 287. Cf. Shakespeare, *Comedy of Errors,* I.i.98: "For we may pity, though not pardon thee"; *Romeo and Juliet,* III.i.202: "Mercy but murders, pardoning those that kill." Knight, p. 289, suggests that Artegall's checking of Talus indicates a new relationship between them. Cf. Jehovah's restraint of the death angel in 1 Chron. 21:15.

15. Cited as significant in Spenser's definition of courtesy by K. Williams, *Spenser's World of Glass,* p. 145, and Lerch, p. 168.

16. *The Education of a Christian Prince,* trans. Lester K. Born (New York: Columbia Univ. Press, 1936), p. 209.

17. Sidney, *Apology,* pp. 151–52, cited by MacIntyre, pp.

10–11. See also Bayley's citation of Thomas Wilson's reference to Orpheus in *The Arte of Rhetorique,* pp. 193–94.

6 · *The Private-to-Public Movement*

1. See Berger's citations of criticism concerning Guyon (p. 3). Criticism is even more unanimous on the other fairy heroes.

2. Berger characterizes Guyon's wisdom as "connatural, virtually instinctive, evoked as a push-button response" to Mammon's arguments (p. 20).

3. The central passage distinguishing the moral natures of the humans and fairies is II.x, the Briton and Elfin Chronicles. The fairies, as Berger remarks, have never fallen and, as a consequence, undergo no internal moral struggle and have no need— or indeed capacity—for redemption (pp. 107–11). Jerry Leath Mills in "Spenser's Emblem of Temperance: Four Studies in *The Faerie Queene,* II.ix–x" (Ph.D. diss., Harvard, 1968), chap. 4, provides an analysis of the chronicles that supports this point. I am aware that Guyon's quest has been discussed as a fictional education—most notably by Maurice Evans, *ELH* 28 (1961):215–24—but Berger's and Mills's analyses seem to me conclusive.

4. See also v.Pro.10–11 and II.x.39 ("Then made he [Donwallo] sacred lawes, which some men say / Were vnto him reueald in vision").

5. The Temple of Venus in Book IV is an apparent exception, but the Temple exemplifies a conception of love as a cosmic force that comprehends the separate virtues of Books III and IV. The hermaphrodite Venus belongs to both books.

6. Pp. 191–92. See also R. F. Hill, "Colin Clout's Courtesy," *Modern Language Review* 57 (1962):498.

7. *Humanism and the Social Order in Tudor England* (Chicago: Univ. of Chicago Press, 1954), p. 191.

8. John Dickerson, *Death of a Republic: Politics and Political Thought at Rome, 59–44 B.C.,* ed. George Lee Haskins (New York: Macmillan, 1963), p. 297. Dickerson cites *De officiis,* I.ix.14; *De legibus,* I.xiii.35, xv.43.

9. Hamlet's speech to Horatio expresses the relation between

temperance and friendship: "Give me that man / That is not passion's slave, and I will wear him / In my heart's core, ay, in my heart of heart, / As I do thee" (III.ii.76—79).

10. By *link* I mean an episode that relates the books both fictionally and thematically. Cf. Knight, pp. 267—69, who considers as thematically anticipatory of Book V Neptune's judgment concerning Florimell (IV.xii), illustrating equity in the distribution of contested property, and regards as a fictional link the wedding in Book V of Florimell, as well as the continued love relationship of Britomart and Artegall.

11. "The Truancy of Calidore," *ELH* 19 (1952):148.

12. Artegall mediates between Amidas and Placidas (V.iv), but he achieves justice, not the reconciliation of opponents as in the cases cited above. The one instance in Book V of the reconciliation of opponents is the mediation between Artegall and Braggadocchio (V.iii) by Guyon, hero of Book II.

13. Roche, p. 119; Frye, p. 115. See also Evans, *Spenser's Anatomy of Heroism,* p. 180.

14. Mohinimohan Bhattacherje makes this point in *Variorum,* 5:287. Plato distinguishes the personal and public aspects of justice in *The Republic,* IV.xvii.

15. *Works,* ed. Frederick J. Furnivall and Sir Israel Gollancz (London: Early English Text Society, 1892—1925), 3:143—44.

16. The susceptibility of prudence to treatment as a public virtue is evident from Aquinas's discussion (*Summa Theologica,* I—II, q. 57, art. 5): "the goal of prudence is in the active principle, whose activity is its perfection: for prudence is right reason about things to be done." See also Steadman, pp. 10—11. If fortitude were designated for Book VIII, as I have suggested, and prudence for Book XI, fortitude though public in relation to the preceding six-book grouping could be treated as private in relation to prudence by Spenser's emphasizing also the medieval conception of fortitude as inner patience. The Letter to Raleigh in fact associates Rinaldo (the irascible passion, according to Tasso's preface to *Gerusalemme Liberata,* and therefore essential to fortitude) with private virtue and Godfrey (the intellectual faculty, according to Tasso, and therefore relative to prudence) with *Politice.*

7 · *Variety and the Moral Dialectic*

1. Notice the nonpejorative citations of *redundant* included in the O.E.D. definitions, as well as the currency of paranomasia and other pleonastic figures in Renaissance poetic theory and practice (including Spenser's own).

2. Joel Elias Spingarn, *A History of Literary Criticism in the Renaissance* (New York: Columbia Univ. Press, 1897), p. 50.

3. The modern tendency to discuss the pictorial effects of *The Faerie Queene* without reference to the moral allegory is challenged by Rudolf Gottfried, "The Pictorial Element in Spenser's Poetry," *ELH* 19 (1952):210, and Lyle Glazier, "The Nature of Spenser's Imagery," *Modern Language Quarterly* 16 (1955):300–310, as well as by Rosamund Tuve, *Allegorical Imagery,* passim. In this regard see also Gottfried's more recent article "Our New Poet: Archetypal Criticism and *The Faerie Queene,*" *PMLA* 83 (1968):1362–77.

4. These identifications have been established by Elkin Calhoun Wilson, *England's Eliza* (1939; rpt., New York: Octagon, 1966), chap. 8. For Elizabeth as Una, see Frank Kermode, *"The Faerie Queene*, I and V," p. 132, and Lawrence Rosinger, *"Spenser's Una and Queen Elizabeth,"* *English Language Notes* 6 (1968):12–17; as Britomart, Edwin Greenlaw, "Spenser's Fairy Mythology," *Studies in Philology* 15 (1918):119–20; as Astraea, Frances A. Yates, "Elizabeth as Astraea," *Journal of the Warburg and Courtauld Institute* 10 (1947):27–82, Roy C. Strong, "The Popular Celebration of the Accession Day of Queen Elizabeth I," *Journal of the Warburg and Courtauld Institute* 21 (1958):86–103, and Alastair Fowler, *Spenser and the Numbers of Time,* pp. 196–200; as Mercilla, Kermode, *"The Faerie Queene*, I and V," p. 143, and William Nelson, *"Queen Elizabeth, Spenser's Mercilla and a Rusty Sword,"* *Renaissance News* 18 (1965):113–17.

5. Tuve's account seems to me more convincing than Greenlaw's association of multiple embodiments of essences in concrete particulars with Plato's ideas (*Variorum,* 1:351). Of course, the method of representing essences by particular facets did not begin in medieval times but was used by Cicero and, earlier, by Aristotle.

6. *Allegorical Imagery*, pp. 119ff. Tuve, p. 127, also suggests a connection between this method of exposition and the notion, expressed by Milton in *Areopagitica*, that since the Fall man must learn good *by* evil.

7. *Allegorical Imagery*, p. 126; Glazier, "The Struggle Between Good and Evil in the First Book of *The Faerie Queene*," *College English* 11 (1950):384.

8. Tuve (*Allegorical Imagery*, p. 106) distinguishes between characters that image the essence of a virtue or vice (e.g., Duessa, who "mirrors falsity pure") and those that image an aspect or represent simply an instance of it. Frye has observed that "virtues are contrasted not only with their vicious opposites, but with vices that have similar names and appearances" (p. 119).

9. Duessa serves the additional function of counterfeiting the idea represented diversely in Una and Fidelia (she calls herself Fidessa, 1.ii.26). Lucifera and Philotime have been associated by Rathborne, pp. 145, 216; see also Kermode, "The Cave of Mammon," in *Elizabethan Poetry*, ed. John Russell Brown and Bernard Harris (London: Arnold, 1960), pp. 160–61.

10. As female lust, however, Malecasta is a counterfeit of female love, which Britomart also represents.

11. H. C. Chang in *Allegory and Courtesy in Spenser: A Chinese View* (Edinburgh: Edinburgh Univ. Press, 1955), pp. 171ff., argues that the enemy of courtesy in Book VI is courtliness. We must not, however, confuse the vicious courtliness of Briana and Mirabella with the genuine courtly demeanor of Calidore. In both Books III and VI the central virtue is opposed by a courtly travesty: courtly love and "courtesy."

12. On the association of the male with reason and the female with passion in Renaissance thought, see Fredson Bowers, "Adam, Eve, and the Fall in *Paradise Lost*," *PMLA*, 84 (1969):265. See also Ambrose, *Paradise* 12–14, 42:294–96, cited in chapter 2.

8 · *Avatars*

1. These episodes are compared by Cheney, pp. 128–36, in relation to their significant differences, as supporting a progression of thought.

2. The two systems also come together in the quest of the first book, which culminates not only in the slaying of the dragon but also in the marriage of Red Cross and Una.

3. Douglas D. Waters, "Duessa and Orgoglio: Red Crosse's Spiritual Fornication," *Renaissance Quarterly* 20 (1967):211–20, interprets the erotic imagery as signifying the act of fornication and, allegorically, spiritual apostasy.

4. Dallett, pp. 109–10, regards the procession of the Seven Deadly Sins as an iconographical paradigm for the representation of their ideas.

5. Green carries a similar meaning in the description of the tapestries of the House of Busirane (III.xi.28), in which, however, the sinister aspect is imaged in the comparison of the gold threads, intermingled with the green, to the half-hidden markings of a serpent lurking within the grass. Also, of Lust it is said, "His wast was with a wreath of yuie greene / Engirt about, ne other garment wore" (IV.vii.7).

6. The offspring of Typhon and Echidna are Orthrus (V.x.10) and the Blatant Beast (VI.vi.9–12); of Typhon (with earth), Ollyphant and Argante (III.vii.47–48); of Echidna (without specification of sire), Geryoneo's Monster (V.xi.23). Orgoglio and Disdain are children of Earth and Aeolus (cf. I.vii.9 and VI.vii.41), in keeping with their allegorical signification. On Typhon and the offspring of his union with Echidna see S. K. Heninger, "The Orgoglio Episode in *The Faerie Queene*," *ELH* 26 (1959):183–86. On the relation of Spenser's serpent to biblical serpents as interpreted by Renaissance commentaries see John E. Hankins, "Spenser and the Revelation of St. John," *PMLA* 60 (1945):373, and John M. Steadman, "Spenser's Errour and the Renaissance Allegorical Tradition," *Neuphilologische Mitteilungen* 62 (1961):22–38.

7. Cleopolis itself as Troynovant, the recapitulation of a succession of ancient civilizations, may be regarded as a kind of historical avatar of the imperial idea. Rathborne, pp. 104–128; Frye, p. 124. The *translatio imperii* topos is traced by Curtius, pp. 28–30.

9 · *Counterpoint and Counterfeit*

1. I am including in *situation* such objects as castles and other edifices, since they pose a challenge as situations for the questing knight.

2. The dragon crest is part of Arthur's description by Geoffrey of Monmouth (*Variorum,* 1:251); but this fact is not a sufficient explanation for its inclusion by Spenser, since he omits a good many other of Geoffrey's details and adds a number of his own.

3. Lerch, pp. 137–38. On Osiris vs. Typhon, see Hankins, *Source and Meaning in Spenser's Allegory* (Oxford: Clarendon, 1971), pp. 77–78.

4. The word *bower,* in Spenser's time as in Chaucer's, meant "bedroom" as well as "arbor."

5. Frye, pp. 121–22. He also cites the wounding of Marinell and Timias in the thigh and the funeral rites of Marinell as part of the Adonis motif.

6. Calidore, to be sure, is not human, and the disappearance of the vision on Mount Acidale may be attributed to his fairy nature, as I have done. Nevertheless the broken vision is, like that of Red Cross, all we are permitted as readers to see.

7. The Castle Joyeous, apart from the belligerence of Malecasta's knights, excludes the darker consequences of the vice it exemplifies, which (as C. S. Lewis has observed) appear later in the House of Busirane, and may be regarded as a kind of anteroom to Busirane's chamber of horrors (p. 340). Cf. Spenser's separation of the dark conclusion and enticing beginning of temptation in Book II with Mordant and Verdant.

8. C. S. Lewis, *Spenser's Images of Life,* ed. Alastair Fowler (Cambridge: Cambridge Univ. Press, 1967), pp. 71–73.

9. Hankins, "Spenser and the Revelation of St. John," p. 377, delineates this contrast.

10. Braggadocchio asks Belphoebe why she permits her beauty to be hidden by the forest from the general view (II.iii.39).

11. Kellogg and Steele edition, p. 27. Though Errour is not precisely a counterfeit since it does not entice Red Cross as a good, we may regard it as a prototype of all the embodiments of evil, both overt and covert, in the poem. Its body of a woman and tail

of a reptile represent the hypocritical character of evil that appears thereafter in images of the counterfeit. It belongs to the iconography of guile.

10 · *Architectonic and Organic Unity*

1. Knight, p. 293. Knight also suggests the unifying function of embodiments of true and false mercy—Mercilla and her opposites, Radigund and Duessa—which are simultaneously images of Elizabeth and Mary, Queen of Scots (pp. 286–87).

2. Cheney, pp. 192–93. Frye compares "Radigund the Amazon in Book V, who rebels against justice, and Mirabella in Book VI, who rebels against courtesy" (p. 125).

3. Frye, p. 117, suggests a similar scheme but does not include the temples of Venus and Isis, since he assumes the Court of Mercilla to be the allegorical core of Book V.

4. Frye, p. 126, includes Malfont and the Blatant Beast in making this point. The image and its iconographic associations derive from Ovid's story of Mercury and Herse.

5. Dallett, pp. 112–19, discusses the light symbolism in relation to the moral allegory.

6. Fulke Greville, *The Life of Sir Philip Sidney* (Oxford: Clarendon, 1907), p. 15.

7. E.g., by the romantic critics and, recently, Frye, who contends that "one cannot begin to discuss the allegory without using the imagery, but one could work out an exhaustive analysis of the imagery without ever mentioning the allegory" (p. 112).

Conclusion · *Critical Justice and the Giant's Faction*

1. *Peacock's Memoirs of Shelley,* ed. H.F.B. Brett-Smith (London: Frowde, 1909), p. 162, n.

2. "Donne and the 1920's: A Problem in Historical Consciousness," *ELH* 27 (1960):25.

3. The numerological system has no meaning without a conceptual structure to engage it.

INDEX

Irascible and concupiscible passions, 65, 68, 101, 141, 143, 168, 210 (n. 16)

Ireland. *See* Irena

Irena, 86; kingdom of, 31, 77–79, 85, 119–20, 121

Irony, 144–45, 147, 160, 174

Isis, 114–17; Temple of, 93, 114–16, 128, 148, 151, 167. *See also* Britomart

Jones, H.S.V., 66

Jove, 34; sword of, 27, 88–89, 127; daughters of, 93

Jusserand, J. J., 42

Justice, 79–82, 95–96, 113–19, 133–35; infused, 127–30; defined by antitypes, 148, 151

Kaske, Robert, 135

Keightley, Thomas, 43–44

Knight, W. Nicholas, 215 (n. 1)

Leicester, Robert Dudley, Earl of, 4–5, 11

Lerch, Christie, 165, 173, 205 (nn. 18, 20), 207 (n. 37); on nature of justice, 79, 80, 81, 129, 206 (n. 28); on Mercilla's court, 93; on Temple of Isis, 114, 148

Letter to Raleigh, 47, 49, 58, 210 (n. 16); importance of to perception of unity, 3–12 passim, 188–89; validity of, 8–11; description of Arthur in, 15, 29; on the meaning of Arthur's quest, 22, 24; reference to Aristotle in, 41–42, 199 (n. 18); on characters as Elizabeth, 50, 144; distinction of humans and fairies by, 60; recognition of variety by, 141; explanation of avatars in, 144, 152, 158

Levels, structural, 59, 137; reinforced by avatars, 177–79

Lewis, C. S., 214 (n. 7)

Liberality, 93–97

Linking episodes, 60, 65–67, 77–79, 102, 132, 203 (n. 6)

Lipsius, Justus, 51, 83–84, 115, 116–17, 206 (n. 24)

Love: as moral aspiration, 18, 37, 156, 198 (n. 8); quests for, 154–57

Lowell, James Russell, 6, 193 (n. 5)

Lucifera, 54, 64; and Philotime, 144, 173; and Mercilla, 168, 171

Lyonesse, 31

Machiavelli, Niccolò, 52

MacIntyre, Jean, 85, 87, 90–91

MacLure, Millar, 148

Macrobius, 16, 42–43, 47–48, 199–200 (n. 21)

Magnificence, 16–24 passim, 56

Maidenhead, Knights of, 30

Majesty, 95–96

Malecasta, 147; Castle Joyeous of, 172–73, 183, 212 (n. 10)

Malory, Thomas, 9

Mammon, 35, 65, 69; cave of, 170, 173, 177–78

Manners, domain of, 83–84, 92, 97–99

Marriage, necessity of friendship in, 106–7

Martin of Braga, 42

Maxwell, J. C., 132

Medina, 65, 143

Mercilla, 30, 167, 177; court of, 92–97, 117–18, 134–35, 170–71; judgment of Duessa by, 93

Merlin: prophecy of, 30, 32, 33, 61; cave of, 128, 182

Millican, Charles Bowie, 197 (n. 5)
Mills, Jerry Leath, 199 (n. 18), 209 (n. 3)
Milton, John, 69, 212 (n. 6)
Mirabella, 163–64, 173
Moral ideal, attainability of, 15, 18
Mordant, 24, 65, 157
Moulton, John Fletcher, Lord, 92, 99
Muses, 36–37
Muzio, Giralomo, 141
Mythological structures, 70

Nature, norm of, 73, 110
Nelson, William, 8, 11, 102, 196 (n. 1)
Neoplatonism, 40, 53
New Criticism. *See* Criticism, formalist
New Jerusalem, vision of, 54–55, 68–69, 125–26, 181–82
Nurture, 25–27, 44

Obedience, Elizabethan homily on, 81
Opposites, definition by, 144–48, 165–66
Oppositions, symbolic, 180–83
Orgoglio, 64, 65, 144, 160, 161, 169; castle of, 170
Origen, 40, 197 (n. 7)
Orpheus, 121
Osgood, C. G., 70
Ovid, 215 (n. 4)
Owen, W.J.B., 4, 5, 70

Padelford, Frederick, 66–67, 145
Palingenius, 39–40
Palmer, 66, 101–2, 129
Paradise, earthly, 36–41, 43–44, 179; false, 103–4, 161, 168–69
Pastorella, 27, 86–87

Paul, 40, 49, 55, 57
Peacock, Thomas Love, 187
Penance, House of, 65
Perceptual and conceptual association, 143–44, 148, 153, 156, 172–73, 183–84.
Phaedria, 69
Phedon, 23
Phillips, James, 208 (n. 10)
Philo, 198 (n. 12)
Philosophy, and poetry, 16
Philotime. *See* Proserpina
Plato, 51, 89, 121, 149, 180, 210 (n. 14), 211 (n. 5)
Pliny, 44
Priamond. *See* Triamond
Pride: and despair, 64–65, 203–4 (n. 9); House of, 160–72, 175
Prosperpina, 144, 146, 173; Garden of, 169
Prudence. *See* Fortitude, and prudence
Pyrochles, 65, 69, 101

Radigund, 116–17, 151, 165, 170, 177
Raleigh, Sir Walter, 31
Rathborne, Isabel, 33
Red Cross, 18, 169, 175, 213 (n. 3); entrance of into Fairyland, 28, 31; and active virtue, 49, 54–57; human identity of, 60–61, 124–26, 128; and Guyon, 63–66, 68–69, 102–4; rescue of by Arthur, 130, 166–72 passim; as opposite of Arthur, 147, 160–61; defeat of by Orgoglio, 160–63, 174
Renwick, William L., 4, 42
Roche, Thomas, Jr., 70, 131, 133
Rose, Mark, 131
Rowse, A. L., 31
Rulers, female, 144, 177, 178
Rymer, Thomas, 3